MW00636239

The Truth about the End Times

Deceived by LIGHT

By Kirk Hille

CONCORDIA PUBLISHING HOUSE • SAINT LOUIS

Schulz

Editor: Mark Sengele

Cover Photo: Brand X Pictures

Your comments and suggestions concerning the material are appreciated. Please write the Editor of Youth Materials, Concordia Publishing House, 3558 S. Jefferson Avenue, St. Louis, MO 63118-3968.

This publication may be available in braille, in large print, or on cassette tape for the visually impaired. Please allow 8 to 12 weeks for delivery. Write to the Library for the Blind, 1333 S. Kirkwood Road, St. Louis, MO 63122-7295; call 1-800-433-3954, ext. 1322; or e-mail to blind.library@lcms.org.

TABLE OF CONTENTS

Introduction

About *Deceived by Light: The Truth about the End Times*

"Don't be deceived, my dear brothers. Every good and perfect gift is from above, coming down from the Father of the heavenly lights, who does not change like the shifting shadows. He chose to give us birth through the word of truth, that we might be a kind of firstfruits of all He created" (James 1:16–18).

Young people today live in a confusing world. Their faith and values are being questioned and confronted by adults and peers alike. Youth are constantly bombarded with information—from the moment they wake until they drop off to sleep. It is difficult to focus on what is important or to know whom to listen to. In His Word, our heavenly Father warned about such distractions and deceptions. The devil himself masquerades as light and tries to lead unsuspecting believers away from the true light of Christ. But, thanks be to God, who gives us His Word and empowers us by His Holy Spirit to resist the devil's deceptions.

Why This Study?

God uses His Word to strengthen and build us up in faith. "Blessed is the one who reads the words of this prophecy, and blessed are those who hear it and take to heart what is written in it, because the time is near" (Revelation 1:3). It is with these words of promise that John begins his account of his glimpse into the heavenly realms.

From Eve in the garden to this present time, the devil has tried to distract God's faithful followers from the path Christ has set before them. One of Satan's chief deceptions is to mislead believers about what God has promised. Shelves of books and videos have appealed to the Christian marketplace, offering their own, often fictional, account of the end times. Thousands of well-meaning Christians have been caught up in senseless speculation about what the end of time will be like. Much of the detail is unknown, shrouded in the mystery and symbolism of God's revelation. Rather than add to what is unknown, it is best to discern the truth and carefully explore what we have in hand, willing to be content without having all the answers.

"I warn everyone who hears the words of the prophecy of this book: If anyone adds anything to them, God will add to him the plagues described in this book. And if anyone takes words away from this book of prophecy, God will take away from him his share in the tree of life and in the holy city, which are described in this book" (Revelation 22:18–19).

This study is designed to focus on Jesus Christ. Through the study of God's Word, the participants will gain a greater understanding of the Book of Revelation. More important, this study seeks to help the faithful remain focused on the truths found within God's Word.

Preparing to Teach

This study of Revelation seeks to connect the words and images found in Revelation to the rest of Scripture. As a result there are many Scripture references used throughout the study. Whenever only a chapter and verse number appear within parentheses in a lesson, that reference is from the Book of Revelation. A glossary of images and terms used in Revelation can be found at the back of the book.

As you prepare to teach this challenging study, allow adequate preparation time. Read all the text for each session before class time. You may want to assign participants to read the text as a way of preparing for class time. For each class session, make enough copies of the student pages for all the class participants. Wait to distribute the student pages until the time indicated in the leader's directions. An additional resource is the excellent commentary by the Rev. Dr. Louis Brighton on the Book of Revelation in the Concordia Commentary Series.

Each of the eight studies in this book follows a similar format: the lesson focus and a simple outline of the study are provided at the beginning of each lesson. The introductory statements are followed by an opening prayer and detailed leader's directions and reproducible student pages. The leader's materials include a series of commentaries on the Bible text. The leader should summarize this material in order to present the information concerning the Revelation text to students. Following each lesson section are one or more "Try This" activities. These active-learning components are designed to help students better relate to the lesson. Each activity helps students to gain a stronger understanding of the Revelation text by connecting it to real-life experiences. Use the closing prayer to wrap up each lesson.

Basic class supplies should include pens or pencils for each student, blank paper, and a chalkboard or equivalent (whiteboard, newsprint pad and easel) with appropriate chalk or markers. Encourage participants to bring along their own Bibles. Keep a supply of Bibles on hand for visitors or students who do not bring their own. The lesson outline suggests supplies needed for each section of the lesson.

Each study is completely outlined for the leader, including suggested lengths of time recommended for each portion of the study. The suggested times total 50–60 minutes. In some cases, depending on class participation, it may be necessary to use additional time or omit portions of the lesson. Most lessons contain optional activities for extending the lesson or alternate activities within the lesson.

Leader's directions also contain instructions for times when you want to have students work together as a whole group or break out into smaller groups of two to four students. These breakout directions are designed to facilitate more intimate discussions of the material. If your numbers are small, you may choose to ignore these breakout suggestions. In some cases you may wish to have the whole group discuss the topic together instead of breaking into smaller groups.

Most of us perform better when there are no "surprises." To avoid surprises, review each lesson fully, well in advance of its presentation. Materials can then be tailored to your individual students' preferences as well as your own.

Adapting These Studies

Depending on your circumstances, you may wish to split lessons and use them over more than one session. Such adaptations are appropriate, perhaps even necessary, for the best possible results. You may wish to adapt one or more lessons for a youth night, retreat, or lock-in format. It may be necessary to supply additional questions or discussion starters for use by your group in these situations.

Adults and youth—even parents and their teenagers—can study these lessons together. While such classes are rare in most churches, there are certain benefits to discussing matters of faith in inter-generational groups. This is especially true when addressing difficult sections of Scripture.

It is necessary to be sensitive to the needs of youth and adults when leading intergenerational groups.

Provide leadership opportunities for young people and adults. Let adults and youth share reading responsibilities, breakout-group leadership tasks, and response reporting duties.

Facilitate interaction. Unless they have had opportunity to study together before, some youth and adults may be initially reluctant to share answers with one another. Use opening group questions and sharing time to "level the playing field" for youth and adults.

Set a comfort level. Help groups to understand that not everyone will want to share, read aloud for the group, or answer every question. Help groups work toward a level of trust with one another.

1

A Perplexing Apocalypse—
How Do You Read Revelation?

Purpose

Young people have many questions concerning the Book of Revelation. It is important to understand the purpose, unique character, and interpretive challenge of Revelation as an apocalyptic book before students begin their study.

Lesson Outline 1

Activity	Suggested Time	Materials Needed
Opening	2 minutes	None
Why Read Revelation?	5 minutes	Copies of Student Page 1A
What's an Apocalypse? **Try This:** *Ancient TV Archaeology*	10 minutes	VHS tape (optional) None
Where Did It Come From? **Try This:** *Evoking Encouragement*	10 minutes	Bibles Get-well/encouragement cards
What's with the Weird Images? **Try This:** *Collecting Clues*	10 minutes	Bibles Magazines, glue, scissors, notebook/paper
What Do the Words Mean? Clues to Chapter 1	optional activity	Copies of Vocabulary Page 1, Bibles
How Do You Read Revelation? **Try This:** *Modern Metaphors* **Try This:** *Description Depiction* **Try This:** *Interpretation Investigation*	15 minutes	None None Picture, paper, pencil None
What's with the Numbers? Clues to Sum Symbolism **Try This:** *Deciphering Digits*	5 minutes	Copies of Student Page 1B None
Closing	2 minutes	Copies of Student Page 1A

Opening *(2 minutes)*

Welcome students to class and begin with this prayer: "Heavenly Father, since You promised to bless whomever reads and keeps Your revelation, send Your Holy Spirit to open our minds and our hearts so we truly understand and correctly apply the message of Your Word to our lives. In Jesus Christ we pray. Amen."

Why Read Revelation? *(5 minutes)*

Distribute copies of Student Page 1A now, or hold them until the close of the lesson. Students may use this page to record notes from the presentation. Like the other books in the Bible, Revelation has been read and believed by billions of people around the world as part of the revealed Word of God. Revelation is different from any other book in the Bible. As the last book in the Bible, it predicts the culmination of the story of salvation and contains the final instructions of Christ to His followers on earth. Unlike any other book in the Bible, it contains promises both at the beginning and the end to bless whomever reads it, hears it, and takes it to heart:

> *Blessed is the one who reads the words of this prophecy, and blessed are those who hear it and take to heart what is written in it, because the time is near. Revelation 1:3*

> *Behold, I am coming soon! Blessed is he who keeps the words of the prophecy in this book. Revelation 22:7*

Revelation is also more difficult to understand than any other book in the Bible. It has been misunderstood throughout history in a wide variety of ways, resulting in failed predictions, church divisions, fear among believers, and even holy wars. Why? Because Revelation is written in the form of an apocalypse, a type of literature that disappeared the second century after Christ and has not been well understood since.

What's an Apocalypse? *(10 minutes)*

Apocalypse is the English version of the Greek word that begins Revelation: *apokalypsis*. It literally means the "revealing, unveiling, or disclosure" of something divinely hidden, covered, or kept secret. Apocalyptic literature uses highly symbolic, coded language to convey a message that will make little sense to outsiders but is fairly clear to those who know the code. An apocalypse is a book written in the style of Revelation and claiming to reveal God's plan for the future. Apocalyptic literature became popular about two hundred years before Christ and continued to be used for about two hundred years after. This apocalyptic book was written especially to encourage people living under severe conditions and served to remind readers that God would bring justice someday. The message of an apocalypse usually involved an angel sent by God presenting a vision. The vision involves the struggle between good and evil at the end of the world. The account uses very symbolic language and calls on its readers to turn from their sins and trust in God's judgment. The Book of Revelation is similar to other apocalypses in these ways, but is also different from apocalyptic writings outside the Bible in a few important ways. Revelation's author shares his name and assumes readers will know who he is. Revelation refers to itself as a prophecy to be taken as God's Word and centers on Christ rather than generally on God. Revelation depicts God's people with an active role to play in the war against evil; it is hopeful about the future because it is shaped by the past—the victory of Christ, the Lamb who was slain.

Try This: *Ancient TV Archaeology*

Ask students to imagine that archaeologists two thousand years from now have dug up a videotape containing an evening of today's television programs. Most other examples of TV programming have long since been destroyed by wars and disasters. The world has given up television for inter-

active holograms, a totally different form of communication and entertainment. The tape includes students' favorite programs and intense eight- to thirty-second commercials unlike anything seen in nineteen hundred years. Ask, "How might people of the future misunderstand the purpose and message of the program? What images and metaphors would they be unlikely to figure out? What would be the result if they tried to interpret the commercials as a part of the story line of the programs?" (Responses will vary, but could include confusion between the programs and the commercials, the change of story lines and characters, and coming to faulty conclusions due to a lack of understanding.) **As an option, actually record some present-day commercials and programs. View them in class, asking students to evaluate them as if they were future archaeologists.**

Where Did It Come From? *(10 minutes)*

Ask a volunteer to read aloud Revelation 1:1–3. Notice that the whole book is about only one lengthy revelation, though people sometimes mistakenly call it "revelations." The entire message was given by God to Jesus, who sent an angel to reveal it to John. John wrote this revelation as a letter to share with seven churches, from where it spread to the entire Christian church. The seven churches were all located in major cities of the Roman province of Asia (some in modern Europe) and may have been chosen because they represented the entire church.

John does not directly identify himself as the friend, disciple, and apostle of Jesus, and some have argued that Revelation was written by a different person named John because it has a different style and content from the Gospel of John. However, the earliest church historians believed it was the same person, who possibly used various assistants to help him write. The writer clearly assumes that the churches of Asia will know who he is and states that he is writing from the island of Patmos, where historian Eusebius (A.D. 265–340) reports John the apostle was exiled for teaching Christianity around A.D. 95, when most scholars believe Revelation was written.

God gave the revelation, John writes, "to show His servants what must soon take place" (Revelation 1:1; 22:6). The Roman Emperor Domitian (A.D. 81–96) was like other emperors, who demanded that they be worshipped as "lord and god" under penalty of death, and Christians throughout the Roman Empire were facing persecution both from fellow Jews and pagan Romans. In order to encourage those suffering and dying for the Christian faith, God reveals His plan for the world, in which Christ will triumph, evil will be destroyed, and believers will be remembered and rewarded.

Try This: *Evoking Encouragement*

Provide students with a number of different sample get-well and encouragement cards. Have students take a good look at the sample greeting cards. Ask, "What kinds of images do they use? What kinds of language do they use? Why? What would you expect a card of encouragement from God to be like?" (Student answers will vary.)

[handwritten note: X's in Glossary in back of this book]

What's with the Weird Images? *(10 minutes)*

Have a volunteer read Revelation 1:4–20. Although John speaks plainly when he refers to himself, he uses a great deal of symbolic language and many metaphors to describe the appearance of Christ. This is not surprising when we consider that human words were invented to describe our lives on this earth but are inadequate at describing the things of God. The picture John describes seems strange to us, but most of the symbolism is found in and explained by other prophetic visions in Scripture, producing a powerful image of the eternal power and glory of Christ Jesus.

In order to help explain the various symbolism and imagery used in each section of Revelation, a list of "clues" are included in each chapter of this book. These clues are also listed alphabetically in the glossary. Read aloud Revelation 1:4–20 again, this time stopping to consider what each symbol says about Christ and the setting in which Revelation was written.

Try This: *Collecting Clues*

Since Revelation is full of so much symbolic language and strange imagery, it may be helpful to create a classroom set of charts or personal notebook entries to keep track of what all the metaphors mean. Have students make small sketches, cut out magazine pictures, or print out clip-art drawings of each image. Write next to the object chosen what the image may mean. How many images occur more than once? How many can be found elsewhere in the Bible? This project may be used as an ongoing activity throughout this study.

What Do the Words Mean? Clues to Chapter 1 *(optional activity)*

Distribute copies of Vocabulary Page 1 to students. Lead a group discussion using the explanations, which follow, of the terms and images John uses in chapter 1. Have students look up the Scripture references, if time allows, to dig deeper and see examples of similar terms or images found elsewhere in Scripture.

If you prefer to work in small groups, assign each group a number of terms to study. Have small groups report their findings to the whole group as you review the complete list.

Read Revelation 1 again. What did students discover that surprised them?

seven spirits [or sevenfold Spirit] (1:4). The Holy Spirit, who is able to see, understand, and explain all truths (Zechariah 4:2–10; Isaiah 11:2; John 16:13–15; Revelation 4:5).

faithful witness (1:5). Jesus, who reveals the truth about God (John 8:18).

firstborn from the dead (1:5). Jesus is resurrected from the tomb so that we also will rise (Colossians 1:18).

ruler of the kings of the earth (1:5). Jesus has power over all earthly rulers (1 Timothy 6:14–16).

coming with the clouds (1:7). Christ's returning to judge the living and the dead (Matthew 24:30; 1 Thessalonians 4:17).

Alpha and Omega (1:8). Jesus brings about the beginning and the end of the world, represented by the first and last letters of the Greek alphabet (Revelation 1:18; 21:6; 22:13).

Lord's Day (1:10). Sunday, the day when Christians celebrate Christ's resurrection (Acts 20:7).

in the Spirit (1:10). John was set free from the limits of time and space through the power of the Holy Spirit, taken out of the physical world to experience the spiritual world (Revelation 4:2; 17:3; 21:10).

seven golden lampstands (1:12). The seven churches (Revelation 1:20).

white like wool . . . as snow (1:14). Indicates the wisdom, purity, and holiness of the presence of God (Daniel 7:9).

eyes like blazing fire (1:14). Intense, pure, and powerful—the eyes of God (Daniel 10:6; Revelation 2:18; 19:12).

feet like bronze glowing (1:15). Intense, pure, and strong, perhaps reminding readers of the two massive bronze pillars that framed the temple built by Solomon (2 Kings 25:17).

voice was like the sound of rushing waters (1:15). Loud, massive, and powerful—the voice of God (Ezekiel 1:24).

seven stars (1:16). Angels (Revelation 1:20).

His right hand (1:16). God's hand of justice and might upholds the angels of the seven churches, indicating that He is protecting them (Exodus 15:6).

double-edged sword (1:16). God's Word, with the power to judge and restore (Ephesians 6:17; Hebrews 4:12).

face like the sun (1:16). Having the glory of God, blinding to the human eye (Revelation 21:23).

Living One (1:18). Not a pagan, dead god, but a God who lives for all eternity (Joshua 3:10; Psalm 42:2; 84:2).

Hades (1:18). The place of the dead, the Greek word for hell (Matthew 16:18).

How Do You Read Revelation? *(15 minutes)*

How do we know which statements in Revelation are symbolic and which are literal? If they are symbolic, how do we know what the symbols represent? The fact is, we can't always know for sure. In fact, there are library shelves full of books with imaginative speculations and interpretations concerning the meaning of this material. However, by applying some basic rules, students can get a clearer understanding of Scripture. These rules are especially important when it comes to interpreting apocalyptic literature such as Revelation. Use the following information to guide your students to a better understanding of how to read and comprehend Revelation.

Use clear passages of Scripture to interpret unclear passages. People throughout history have developed elaborate schemes based on the unclear passages of Revelation and Daniel to try to predict the date on which the world will end. Yet this is not what Scripture clearly states elsewhere:

> *No one knows about that day or hour, not even the angels in heaven, nor the Son, but only the Father. As it was in the days of Noah, so it will be at the coming of the Son of Man. Matthew 24:36-37*

> *No one knows about that day or hour, not even the angels in heaven, nor the Son, but only the Father. Be on guard! Be alert! You do not know when that time will come. Mark 13:32-33*

> *You also must be ready, because the Son of Man will come at an hour when you do not expect Him. Luke 12:40*

> *Now, brothers, about times and dates we do not need to write to you, for you know very well that the day of the Lord will come like a thief in the night. 1 Thessalonians 5:1-2; see also 2 Peter 3:10*

Based on these clear passages of Scripture, we can assume that Christ could return at any time, regardless of whether or not He has been predicted to return!

Try This: *Modern Metaphors*

Have students make a list of as many common metaphors and symbolic phrases as they can think of in three minutes. For example: go jump in a lake, green with envy, muscle cars burning rubber, hot chicks hanging out. Ask, "What does each phrase really mean? How do we know that these phrases are not to be understood literally?" (Phrases have a variety of mean-

ings. In order to understand the expression, you need to understand the language or context in which the expression occurs.)

Recognize that prophetic visions mix, and even overlap, events that are near and far away in time. Apocalyptic writings do not always present events in the order they will occur, though people often try to understand them that way. For instance, when Isaiah proclaimed "The virgin will be with child and will give birth to a son, and will call him Immanuel" (Isaiah 7:14), he may have expected that this prophecy was soon fulfilled when his wife had a son (Isaiah 8:3), since the topic of the prophecy seemed to be the time of Israel's exile. Yet Matthew later recognized the prediction as applying to a much later event—the birth of Jesus (Matthew 1:22–23). Jesus Himself seemed to mix and overlap near and far future events when describing the end times to His disciples (Matthew 24). This overlapping of prophetic visions is sometimes called prolepsis. We do a similar thing when we describe a picture, going from left to right or top to bottom, sometimes describing the same object more than once; rather than describing the objects in order from those that appear closest to those that appear farthest away.

Try This: *Description Depiction*

Have two volunteers sit back-to-back. Give one volunteer a picture of a busy scene with a variety of simple objects in it. Give the other volunteer paper and a pencil to sketch the objects described from the picture by the first volunteer. Silently observe the order in which the first volunteer describes the objects in the picture and the words used to describe the objects' relationship to one another. Ask the students how the volunteers approached their task. Did the description move from objects that are close to far, far to close, right to left, left to right, top to bottom, bottom to top, in a circle, or in some other manner? What difference did the order in which the objects were described make in how the person sketching interpreted them? How would the picture look if the person describing the objects didn't say how they are related?

Don't take symbolic language literally. When Peter asked Jesus, "Lord, how many times shall I forgive my brother when he sins against me? Up to seven times?" Jesus answered, "I tell you, not seven times, but seventy-seven times" (Matthew 18:21–22). Jesus did not mean that we should keep track, and on the 78th time refuse to forgive. The disciples understood Jesus to mean that we should always forgive anyone who repents. They knew this because in Jesus' day, and throughout Scripture, the number seven was used symbolically to mean a complete time, just as seven days make a complete week. "Seventy-seven times" (or literally seven times seventy) was a symbolic way of saying "always" in a culture that did not yet have a distinct mathematical sign for infinity. When the literal meaning of a phrase doesn't make sense compared to the rest of Scripture and a symbolic understanding fits better, the meaning is probably meant symbolically.

Don't take literal language symbolically. Jesus ordered His disciples "not to tell anyone what they had seen until the Son of Man had risen from the dead. They kept the matter to themselves, discussing what 'rising from the dead' meant" (Mark 9:9–10). Later the disciples were surprised to find Jesus' tomb empty, even though He had told them what would happen and had raised others from the dead. They thought Jesus was speaking symbolically when He was speaking literally (John 2:22). If the literal meaning of a phrase makes sense and matches what we know of God's plan from the rest of Scripture, it may be taken literally.

To decide what is meant in a passage that seems symbolic, look at how the same image is used other places. The primary source would be in the same book; if not there, then we turn elsewhere in Scripture. A secondary source may be the history and culture in which the book was written. The stars John sees in Revelation 1:16 are explained to represent angels in Revelation 1:20. The river of the water of life John sees in Revelation 22:1 is an image used by Jeremiah, Zechariah, and Jesus, which John 7:38–39 explains as representing the Holy Spirit. The seven hills on which a woman sits in Revelation 17:9 would remind John's readers of Rome, since cities were often compared to women in ancient cultures (2 Kings 19:21), and history records Rome as being famous for its location on seven hills.

Try This: *Interpretation Investigation*

List each of these possible interpretations on the board or newsprint; then cover them so that you can reveal one at a time after reading the sentence given below.

■ Your father was literally on fire for exactly 240 months, then smothered the flames with a frozen turkey at the time a friend created cancer for the lungs.

■ Someone like a father to you burned with rage for what seemed like a score of years, but his anger ceased as quickly as a turkey can die when a friend began to breathe out deadly, cancerous threats.

■ Your father had 20 years' experience smoking meats, but stopped smoking turkey at low temperatures when a friend developed lung cancer as a result.

■ After two dispensations of history, the father of lies, Satan, will leave hell to cool the hearts of believers and afflict them with turkey-like ignorance as corruption cuts off the breath of the church.

■ My dad smoked cigarettes for 20 years. He quit smoking suddenly and without special assistance when he heard that a friend had been diagnosed with lung cancer.

Read the following sentence aloud: "A smoker for 20 years, my dad quit cold turkey when a friend developed lung cancer."

Reveal the possible interpretations one at a time. Allow student to discuss each interpretation. Ask, "What mistakes have been made in interpretation? What does the sentence really mean? How do we know?" (The phrase was taken too literally, too figuratively, or out of context. We understand the phrase within the context it was spoken.)

What's with the Numbers? Clues to Sum Symbolism *(5 minutes)*

Distribute copies of Student Page 1B. The information that follows may be used to lead a discussion with the students as they complete the Student Page.

In Revelation, as in much of the Bible, certain numbers keep appearing over and over again. People in biblical times used symbolic numbers to convey certain meanings, much as people do today. We would rather be considered a "10" than a "zero," and would rather be a "4.0" than "2nd" string or a "5th" wheel. In the Bible, and especially in Revelation, the following sums have important meanings:

3. The number of God (the Holy Trinity: Father, Son, and Holy Spirit; the same yesterday, today, and forever) or evil trying to displace God through an unholy trinity.

3½. The number of evil and brokenness (broken perfection, half the perfect number 7); often used to describe an evil time, as in 3½ years, the equivalent of 42 months or 1,260 days.

4. The number of the earth (4 directions, 4 seasons, 4 corners of the earth).

6. The number of evil and incompleteness (1 less than 7), and perhaps the number to represent humanity, created on the 6th day. Great evil is 666 (the number of evil or humankind trying to appear triune, like God).

7. The number of completion and absolute perfection or holiness (7 days of creation, 7 days in a week, the 7th day devoted to worship), or the reunion of God with the earth (3 + 4) through a covenant of grace.

10. The number of completion and perfection (10 fingers, 10 toes) brought about by God (3 + 7), including the cube of 10 (1,000) for absolute completion and perfection.

12. The number representing God's people (12 tribes, 12 disciples), God at work on the earth (3 x 4), including multiples such as 12,000 and 144,000 for the church made complete.

Try This: *Deciphering Digits*

List these digits on the board or newsprint: 1, 13, 21, 10-4, 7-11, 360, 911, 1040, 20/20, 24/7/365. Ask students, "What meanings do these digits imply in our culture? What are some other sets of digits that mean more than just a number? How did they come to mean these things?" (Answers will vary.)

Closing *(2 minutes)*

If you have not yet distributed copies of Student Page 1A, do so now. These sheets may be completed by students at home for a review of the lesson. Close with prayer:

"Almighty God, human language is hard-pressed to tell about the awesome wonders of Your love and Your plan for humankind. Help us, through the power of Your Holy Spirit, to recognize and share with others the greatness of Your glory and sureness of Your salvation. In Jesus Christ we pray. Amen."

A Perplexing Apocalypse—How Do You Read Revelation?

Why Read Revelation?

What's an Apocalypse?

This English version of the Greek word that begins Revelation means

This ancient style of writing, full of symbolic imagery, is designed to encourage

How is Revelation similar to other apocalypses outside Scripture?

How is Revelation different from other apocalypses outside Scripture?

Where Did It Come From? (Revelation 1:1–3)

Who gave the revelation to John? Whom did John give it to?

Why do most people think this John is the same person who wrote the Gospel of John?

Why did the early Christians need the encouragement Revelation provides?

How Do You Read Revelation?

Interpret unclear passages of Scripture based on the _____ passages.

Recognize that prophetic visions mix, and even overlap, events near and far away in _____.

They do not always present events in the order they will occur.

Don't take symbolic language _____. If the literal meaning of a phrase doesn't make sense when compared to the rest of Scripture, a symbolic understanding may fit better.

Don't take literal language _____. If the literal meaning of a phrase makes sense and matches what we know of God's plan from the rest of Scripture, it may be meant literally.

To decide what symbolic language means, look at how the same image is used other places in the

book, elsewhere in _____, and in the history and _____ in which the book is written.

What's with the Numbers?

3 =

3½ =

4 =

6 =

7 =

10 =

12 =

What Do the Words Mean? (Revelation 1:4–20)

seven spirits **(1:4) Zechariah 4:2–10; Isaiah 11:2; John 16:13–15; Revelation 4:5**

faithful witness **(1:5) John 8:18**

firstborn from the dead **(1:5) Colossians 1:18**

ruler of the kings of the earth **(1:5) 1 Timothy 6:14–16**

coming with the clouds **(1:7) Matthew 24:30; 1 Thessalonians 4:17**

Alpha and Omega **(1:8) Revelation 21:6; 22:13**

Lord's Day **(1:10) Acts 20:7**

in the Spirit **(1:10) Revelation 4:2; 17:3; 21:10**

seven golden lampstands **(1:12) Revelation 1:20**

white like wool . . . as snow **(1:14) Daniel 7:9**

eyes like blazing fire **(1:14) Daniel 10:6; Revelation 2:18; 19:12**

feet like bronze glowing **(1:15) 2 Kings 25:17**

voice was like the sound of rushing waters **(1:15) Ezekiel 1:24**

seven stars **(1:16) Revelation 1:20**

His right hand **(1:16) Exodus 15:6**

double-edged sword **(1:16) Ephesians 6:17; Hebrews 4:12**

face like the sun **(1:16) Revelation 21:23**

Living One **(1:18) Joshua 3:10; Psalm 42:2; 84:2**

Hades **(1:18) Matthew 16:18**

REVELATION 2–3

Challenging the Church—
How Do We Live While We Wait?

Purpose

Through their study of Revelation, young people will learn to recognize and respond to Christ's care for, and challenges to, His church.

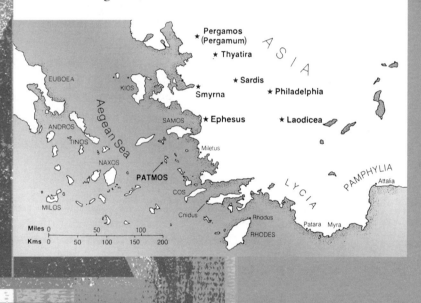

Activity	Suggested Time	Materials Needed
Opening	2 minutes	None
Who Are the Seven Churches? **Try This:** *Chart the Churches*	20 minutes	Bibles Copies of Student Page 2A
What Is Jesus Saying? **Try This:** *Lengthen the List*	30 minutes	Copies of Student Page 2A Copies of Student Page 2A
What Do the Words Mean? Clues to Chapters 2–3 **Try This:** *Repentance Response*	optional activity	Copies of Vocabulary Page 2, Bibles Copies of Student Page 2B
Closing	2 minutes	None

Opening *(2 minutes)*

Lord of Life, send Your Spirit to speak to us in Your church today that we might turn from our sins and serve You until You return to end all evil and reward the faithful. Through Jesus Christ we pray. Amen.

Who Are the Seven Churches? *(20 minutes)*

Read Revelation 2–3. The seven churches Christ speaks to in Revelation 2 and 3 are seven real congregations located in major cities of the Roman province of Asia Minor (around present-day Turkey). Yet these seven also represent the entire body of believers for whom Christ's revelation is intended, since after each letter Christ proclaims, "He who has an ear, let him hear what the Spirit says to the churches" (Revelation 2:7, 11, 17, 29; 3:6, 13, 22).

It is unclear why the letters are addressed "to the angel" of each church. The word *angel* comes from the Greek *angelos*, which can mean simply "messenger." However, every time "angel" is used in Revelation, it indicates a spirit serving God. Whether or not these are the same seven angels who announce and enact God's judgment later in Revelation is unknown. Their job here is to make sure the message gets through to each church, just as Christ made the entire book known "by sending His angel" (Revelation 1:1).

The seven letters follow a similar pattern, causing their similarities and differences to stand out. In each letter Christ addresses a congregation using one or more of His titles. The Lord assures them that He knows their situation, commends what good they have done, challenges them to repent of their failures or to persevere in the faith, and then promises a reward "to him who overcomes." In every case, the power to overcome is graciously given by Christ Himself through His victory and forgiveness won on the cross. The specific situation, title, commendation, challenge, and description of reward offered by Christ varies with each congregation.

Try This: *Chart the Churches*

Distribute copies of Student Page 2A. Allow students to work in small groups. Have each group reread Revelation 2–3. Have students use Student Page 2A to chart what Christ calls Himself, what He commends, what He challenges, and what He promises in the case of each congregation. The section that follows may be used to review students' findings.

What Is Jesus Saying? *(30 minutes)*

The information that follows is a summary of the situations in each of the seven churches and the promises Christ gives the entire church through them. You may use this section as a review of the "Chart the Churches" activity or as a discussion/presentation. Provide students with copies of Student Page 2A so that they may record their own notes/insights.

Enduring Ephesus *(Revelation 2:1–7)*

Where It Is: A busy, wealthy seaport on the main highway between Jerusalem and Rome, Ephesus boasted a temple of the pagan goddess Diana that was one of the seven wonders of the ancient world as well as a center for prostitution and emperor worship. Paul stayed in Ephesus almost three years helping establish its important church, leaving Timothy in charge when he departed. Later, John the Apostle was a pastor of this church, which had become so influential and evangelistic that Jesus chides them, "Remember the height from which you have fallen!" (Revelation 2:5).

How Christ Is Described: Him who holds seven stars, walks among lampstands (i.e., the Lord of the churches).

What's Right: The church is hardworking, persevering, intolerant of the wicked, discerning of false apostles, enduring of hardships, hating immoral Nicolaitans.

What's Wrong: They have turned away their first love, substituting busyness for passion in their relationship with Christ.

What's Promised to the Faithful: The right to eat from the tree of life (immortality).

Suffering Smyrna *(Revelation 2:8–11)*

Where It Is: A prosperous harbor town 35 miles north of Ephesus on the Aegean Sea, Smyrna built a temple to the Roman Emperor Tiberius in A.D. 26 and had a large stadium. Polycarp, the famous bishop of the poor and persecuted congregation here, would later be martyred by Jews who became so violent in rejecting Christ that they are referred to as "a synagogue of Satan" (Revelation 2:9).

How Christ Is Described: First and Last, who died and rose again.

What's Right: The church is known by Christ and is rich in faith.

What's Wrong: They are poor, afflicted, slandered, afraid.

What's Promised to the Faithful: The crown of (eternal) life, protection from the second death (hell).

Persevering Pergamum *(Revelation 2:12–17)*

Where It Is: About 50–55 miles north of Smyrna, Pergamum boasted another of the seven wonders of the ancient world, a library of 200,000 parchment scrolls. There were also many temples to Roman deities, including a white marble altar to Jupiter on a hill 1,000 feet above the rest of the city, and a temple to the god of healing, Askelepias. The official seat for emperor worship in Asia, Pergamum was so full of idols that Jesus said, "I know where you live— where Satan has his throne" (Revelation 2:13).

How Christ Is Described: Him who has the sharp, double-edged sword (power of God's Word to judge).

What's Right: The church was faithful, even when Antipas is martyred.

What's Wrong: They are tolerant of idol worshipers, sexual immorality, and false teachers.

What's Promised to the Faithful: Christ offers hidden manna (bread of life/everlasting life) and a white stone (innocence) with a new name (name of Christ) that would be their inheritance.

Trusty Thyatira *(Revelation 2:18–29)*

Where It Is: A thriving trade center southeast of Pergamum, Thyatira's many craft guilds made it difficult for members to become Christians, since guild membership involved worship of a pagan god and immorality at its festivals. Paul met a businesswoman named Lydia from Thyatira who became his first convert to Christianity in Europe.

How Christ Is Described: Son of God, with eyes like blazing fire and feet like burnished bronze.

What's Right: The church is hardworking, loving, faithful, serving, persevering, and growing in good works.

What's Wrong: They tolerate a false prophetess, who misleads people into sexual immorality and idolatry.

What's Promised to the Faithful: The authority to judge nations, the morning star (light of Christ).

Sleepy Sardis *(Revelation 3:1–6)*

Where It Is: A formerly great city located high on a mountain south of Thyatira, Sardis was famous for manufacturing and dying wool, but was twice captured in surprise attacks because the people thought they were safe. They loved ease, luxury, wealth, and were zealous in emperor worship.

How Christ Is Described: Him who holds the seven spirits and seven stars (the Holy Spirit and the church).

What's Right: They have a good reputation; a few members have refused to compromise beliefs.

What's Wrong: They are actually dead, disobedient, incomplete, half-hearted.

What's Promised to the Faithful: The faithful will be dressed in white, have their name in the book of life, and be acknowledged in heaven.

Feeble Philadelphia *(Revelation 3:7–13)*

Where It Is: A young city founded to spread Greek culture in the regions southeast of Sardis, Philadelphia was destroyed by an earthquake in A.D. 17, but rebuilt. Known as the "Gateway to the East," Philadelphia is described by Christ as "an open door" (Revelation 3:8).

How Christ Is Described: Him who is holy and true, who holds the key of David to open and shut the door.

What's Right: They have good deeds, have kept God's Word, have not denied Christ, have patiently endured, are uniquely loved by Christ.

What's Wrong: The church has little strength, is perhaps afraid.

What's Promised to the Faithful: The faithful will be eternally present in the temple of God and marked with names of God, heaven, and Christ.

Lukewarm Laodicea *(Revelation 3:14–22)*

Where It Is: A very wealthy and proud commercial center at the intersection of two highways 40 miles southeast of Philadelphia, Laodicea was famous for fine black wool, banking, medicinal hot springs, and a medical school that had developed a remedy for weak eyes.

How Christ Is Described: Amen, faithful and true witness, ruler of God's creation.

What's Right: There is nothing mentioned!

What's Wrong: The church is lukewarm, proud, complacent, poor in faith, blind to the needs of others, and spiritually bankrupt.

What's Promised to the Faithful: The right to sit on the throne with Christ.

Try This: *Lengthen the List*

What would Jesus say to your congregation? Have students complete the section provided on Student Page 2A with a short statement about your location and congregation. Ask students to include a title or two for Christ that they consider especially meaningful, a few words describing the strengths of your congregation, and a few words describing weaknesses. Ask, "What is it that Christ offers to everyone who remains faithful and overcomes this world? Which of the seven congregations in Revelation does our congregation most resemble? Why? How do Christ's promises encourage you toward repentance and growth?" (Christ offers eternal life in heaven to all the faithful. Answers will vary.)

What Do the Words Mean? Clues to Chapters 2–3 *(optional activity)*

Distribute copies of Vocabulary Page 2. Work through the explanations of what the terms and images John uses may mean. (Explanations for words are in the glossary.) If time allows, have students look up the Scripture references in order to dig deeper and see examples of similar terms or images found in Scripture.

If you prefer to work in small groups, assign each group a number of terms to study. Have small groups report their findings to the whole group as they review the complete list.

Read Revelation 2–3 again. What do you discover that's new to you?

apostles (2:2). Those sent out with the authority of Christ, including the original 12 apostles and others sent by the church to preach the Good News (Romans 16:7; 2 Corinthians 11:13).

first love (2:4). Passion and priority given to Christ, as when one first falls in love.

remove your lampstand (2:5). Take away the prominent position of the congregation before God (Revelation 1:20).

Nicolaitans (2:6). Followers of Nicolas, who apparently condoned immorality (Revelation 2:15).

tree of life (2:7). The source of immortality and healing (Genesis 2:9; 3:22; Revelation 22:2, 14, 19).

synagogue of Satan (2:9). Jewish people who reject the Christ and persecute Christians (Revelation 3:9).

ten days (2:10). A short, but complete period of time (Genesis 24:55).

crown of life (2:10). A symbol of victory over death (James 1:12).

second death (2:11). Suffering and destruction in hell (Revelation 20:14; 21:8).

where Satan has his throne (2:13). The center of emperor worship and other idolatry.

Antipas (2:13). An otherwise unknown Christian martyr in the church at Pergamum.

Balaam, who taught Balak (2:14). Balaam was infamous as the prophet who helped Balak, king of Moab, in his attempts to curse Israel (Numbers 22:40–25:5; 31:13–16).

hidden manna (2:17). The mysterious bread from heaven that sustained Israel in its desert wanderings; may suggest a secret source of divine strength or Jesus as the bread of life (John 6:30–58).

white stone (2:17). May signify innocence, referring to the custom of judges declaring a person innocent by casting a white stone into an urn.

new name (2:17). Implies belonging and a fresh beginning, as through Baptism we are adopted into God's family (Isaiah 62:2; Revelation 3:12; 22:4).

Jezebel (2:20). A woman of notorious wickedness, she was the idolatrous wife of King Ahab, who introduced the worship of Baal to Israel and killed the true prophets of God (1 Kings 21:25–26).

commit adultery (2:22). Often refers to idolatry, not just sexual immorality (Jeremiah 3:6; Hosea 1:2).

strike her children dead (2:23). Not necessarily literal children, but those who follow her ways (Hosea 2:4).

Satan's so-called deep secrets (2:24). The experience of evils, such as the idolatry and sexual immorality of Jezebel. These were falsely taught by some as necessary to defeat Satan.

iron scepter (2:27). Authority that cannot be broken; predicted of the Messiah (Psalm 2:7–9; Revelation 12:5), claimed by Christ (Revelation 19:15), and shared with His people (Revelation 2:26).

dash them to pieces like pottery (2:27). Quickly judge and easily destroy all that is sinful, as when a potter shatters defective pottery (Psalm 2:7–9; Isaiah 30:12–14).

morning star (2:28). Jesus, whose return brings a new and better time, as the appearance of the morning star signaled to ancient watchmen the arrival of a new day (2 Peter 1:19; Revelation 22:16).

like a thief (3:3). Suddenly and unexpectedly (Matthew 24:42–44; 1 Thessalonians 5:2–4; 2 Peter 3:10; Revelation 16:15).

soiled their clothes (3:4). Intentionally and publicly sinning (Isaiah 64:6; Zechariah 3:3–4).

dressed in white (3:4). Cleansed of sin and covered by Christ's righteousness (Isaiah 61:10; Galatians 3:27; Revelation 7:13–14) and eternal life (1 Corinthians 15:53; 2 Corinthians 5:2–3).

book of life (3:5). God's record of those made righteous and saved from hell (Psalm 69:28; Philippians 4:3; Revelation 13:8; 17:8; 20:12, 15; 21:27).

key of David (3:7). Authority to open or close the kingdom of heaven as the Messiah descended from King David (Revelation 1:18), represented by the same image used to confer authority over Judah to Eliakim (Isaiah 22:20–22).

what He opens . . . shut[s] (3:7). Christ alone can open and close the opportunity for salvation (Isaiah 22:22).

open door (3:8). Opportunity for salvation to spread (1 Corinthians 16:9; 2 Corinthians 2:12; Colossians 4:3) from Philadelphia.

pillar in the temple (3:12). Symbol of strength in the presence of God (1 Kings 7:15–21).

write on him the name (3:12). Confer belonging and character (Revelation 14:1).

new Jerusalem (3:12). Paradise, the dwelling place of believers after the resurrection (Revelation 21:2).

Amen (3:14). True, a Hebrew word used to declare the truthfulness of a statement or person (1 Corinthians 14:16).

lukewarm (3:16). Apathetic, without passion either for or against God. The attitude of the Laodiceans is neither refreshing, like cool water, nor healing, like the hot springs of nearby Hierapolis.

spit you out (3:16). Reject as distasteful (Job 20:15).

wretched, pitiful, poor, blind and naked (3:17). Though Laodiceans were proud of their worldly wealth, vision treatments, and fine wool, they lacked good works, spiritual insight, and the cover of Christ's righteousness.

gold refined (3:18). True righteousness that withstands God's judgment, as pure gold is separated from impurities by extreme heat (1 Corinthians 3:12–15; 1 Peter 1:7).

Try This: *Repentance Response*

Distribute copies of Student Page 2B. Allow students to work alone or together in groups. Share the directions found below, and allow time for students to work. When students have finished, provide time for them to share their letters.

With which of the seven churches can you most identify? Choose one, and imagine that you are the secretary of that congregation. Write a letter or prayer responding to the message Christ sent to that church. For what does your congregation thank the Lord? From what does your congregation intend to turn away? For what does your congregation ask? Remember: It can be easy to find fault with your congregation, since it is made up of sinful people. Yet is it also easy to celebrate forgiveness, since it has been bought for us by Christ. He challenges His churches in order to turn us back to His salvation and the power of His Spirit. Be sure your letter reflects the confidence we have in Jesus' forgiveness and faithful guidance!

Closing *(2 minutes)*

Lord of the church, assure us of Your forgiveness and fill us with the power of Your Spirit so that we can become the congregation You would like us to be and receive the reward You have promised us in heaven. Through Jesus Christ we pray. Amen.

What Is Jesus Saying?

Enduring Ephesus

Where It Is: A busy, wealthy seaport on the main highway between Jerusalem and Rome, Ephesus boasted a temple of the pagan goddess Diana that was one of the seven wonders of the ancient world as well as a center for prostitution and emperor worship. Paul stayed in Ephesus almost three years helping establish its important church, leaving Timothy in charge when he departed. Later, John the Apostle was a pastor of this church, which had become so influential and evangelistic that Jesus chides them, "Remember the height from which you have fallen!" (Revelation 2:5).

How Christ Is Described:

What's Right:

What's Wrong:

What's Promised to the Faithful:

Suffering Smyrna

Where It Is: A prosperous harbor 35 miles north of Ephesus on the Aegean Sea, Smyrna built a temple to the Roman Emperor Tiberius in A.D. 26 and had a large stadium. Polycarp, the famous bishop of the poor and persecuted congregation here, would later be martyred by Jews who became so violent in rejecting Christ that they are referred to as "a synagogue of Satan" (Revelation 2:9).

How Christ Is Described:

What's Right:

What's Wrong:

What's Promised to the Faithful:

Persevering Pergamum

Where It Is: About 50–55 miles north of Smyrna, Pergamum boasted another of the seven wonders of the ancient world, a library of 200,000 parchment scrolls. There were also many temples to Roman deities, including a white marble altar to Jupiter on a hill 1,000 feet above the rest of the city and a temple to the god of healing, Askelepias. The official seat for emperor worship in Asia, Pergamum was so full of idols that Jesus says, "I know where you live—where Satan has his throne" (Revelation 2:13).

How Christ Is Described:

What's Right:

What's Wrong:

What's Promised to the Faithful:

Trusty Thyatira

Where It Is: A thriving trade center southeast of Pergamum, Thyatira's many craft guilds made it difficult for guild members to become Christians, since membership involved worship of a pagan god and immorality at its festivals. Paul met a businesswoman named Lydia from Thyatira who became his first convert to Christianity in Europe.

How Christ Is Described:

What's Right:

What's Wrong:

What's Promised to the Faithful:

Sleepy Sardis

Where It Is: A formerly great city located high on a mountain south of Thyatira, Sardis was famous for manufacturing and dying wool, but was twice captured in surprise attacks because the people thought they were safe. They loved ease, luxury, wealth, and were zealous in emperor worship.

How Christ Is Described:

What's Right:

What's Wrong:

What's Promised to the Faithful:

Feeble Philadelphia

Where It Is: A young city founded to spread Greek culture in the regions southeast of Sardis, Philadelphia was destroyed by an earthquake in A.D. 17, but rebuilt. Known as the "Gateway to the East," Philadelphia is described by Christ as "an open door" (Revelation 3:8).

How Christ Is Described:

What's Right:

What's Wrong:

What's Promised to the Faithful:

Lukewarm Laodicea

Where It Is: A very wealthy and proud commercial center at the intersection of two highways 40 miles southeast of Philadelphia, Laodicea was famous for fine black wool, banking, medicinal hot springs, and a medical school that had developed a remedy for weak eyes.

How Christ Is Described:

What's Right:

What's Wrong:

What's Promised to the Faithful:

My Church

Where We Are:

Who Christ Is to Us:

What's Right:

What's Wrong:

What We Look Forward To:

Repentance Response

Dear _____,

Thank You for

As a congregation, we have decided to

We humbly ask, therefore, that You would

Yours truly,

_____

apostles **(2:2) Romans 16:7; 2 Corinthians 11:13**

first love **(2:4)**

remove your lampstand **(2:5) Revelation 1:20**

Nicolaitans **(2:6) Revelation 2:15**

tree of life **(2:7) Genesis 2:9; 3:22; Revelation 22:2, 14, 19**

synagogue of Satan **(2:9) Revelation 3:9**

ten days **(2:10) Genesis 24:55**

crown of life **(2:10) James 1:12**

second death **(2:11) Revelation 20:14; 21:8**

where Satan has his throne **(2:13)**

Antipas **(2:13)**

Balaam, who taught Balak **(2:14) Numbers 22:40–25:5; 31:13–16**

hidden manna **(2:17) John 6:30–58**

white stone **(2:17)**

new name **(2:17) Isaiah 62:2; Revelation 3:12; 22:4**

Jezebel **(2:20) 1 Kings 21:25–26**

commit adultery **(2:22) Jeremiah 3:6; Hosea 1:2**

strike her children dead **(2:23) Hosea 2:4**

Satan's so-called deep secrets **(2:24)**

iron scepter **(2:27) Psalm 2:7–9; Revelation 12:5; 19:15; 2:26**

dash them to pieces like pottery **(2:27) Psalm 2:7–9; Isaiah 30:12–14**

morning star **(2:28) 2 Peter 1:19; Revelation 22:16**

like a thief **(3:3) Matthew 24:42–44; 1 Thessalonians 5:2–4; 2 Peter 3:10; Revelation 16:15**

soiled their clothes **(3:4) Isaiah 64:6; Zechariah 3:3–4**

dressed in white **(3:4) Isaiah 61:10; Galatians 3:27; Revelation 7:13–14; 1 Corinthians 15:53; 2 Corinthians 5:2–3**

book of life **(3:5) Psalm 69:28; Philippians 4:3; Revelation 13:8; 17:8; 20:12, 15; 21:27**

key of David **(3:7) Revelation 1:18; Isaiah 22:20–22**

what He opens . . . shut[s] **(3:7) Isaiah 22:22**

open door **(3:8) 1 Corinthians 16:9; 2 Corinthians 2:12; Colossians 4:3**

pillar in the temple **(3:12) 1 Kings 7:15–21**

write on him the name **(3:12) Revelation 14:1**

new Jerusalem **(3:12) Revelation 21:2**

Amen **(3:14) 1 Corinthians 14:16**

lukewarm **(3:16)**

spit you out **(3:16) Job 20:15**

wretched, pitiful, poor, blind and naked **(3:17)**

gold refined **(3:18) 1 Corinthians 3:12–15; 1 Peter 1:7**

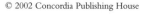

REVELATION 4–5

Revealing the Redeemer—
Where Is Christ in the Chaos?

Purpose

Young and old alike seek to understand the chaotic result of sin in the world. As young people study God's Word in Revelation, they can learn to celebrate and seek Christ's involvement in all of history and in all aspects of life as well.

Activity	Suggested Time	Materials Needed
Opening	2 minutes	None
What's Happening in Heaven? **Try This:** *Spectacle Sharing*	10 minutes	Bibles None

What Do the Words Mean?
    Clues to Chapters 4–5
    Try This: *Site Seeing*
	25 minutes	Copies of Vocabulary Page 3,
		
		Bibles, Construction paper,
		magazines, scissors, glue sticks

Where's God When We Need Him?
    Try This: *Holy Help*
    Try This: *Songs of the Saints*
	15 minutes	Bibles
		Paper, pens/pencils
		Hymnals/songbooks

Closing	2 minutes	None

Do First

Read

Opening *(2 minutes)*

God of the universe, thank You for Your presence in our lives. Send Your Holy Spirit to reassure us of Your power and love. Enable us to worship You even when our world is falling apart. Through Jesus Christ, our victorious Savior, we pray. Amen.

What's Happening in Heaven? *(10 minutes)*

In the first chapter of Revelation, John describes how Christ appeared to him in order to reveal His message of encouragement for the church. In the second and third chapters, John records specific messages Christ sends to seven congregations and, through the preserved message of Scripture, to all believers. Now, in the fourth and fifth chapters, the scene changes as John is taken up in the Spirit to heaven, where he is shown what's happening before God's throne. Ask volunteers to read aloud Revelation 4–5.

Heaven is wonderful but unique beyond description, so John has to use words such as "had the appearance of," and "was like" and "as if." Surrounding God's majestic throne, four awesome angels and 24 great elders from among God's saints continually lead the angels and all creation in worshiping God. John can't begin to describe the Father Himself, but portrays Him as holding a scroll, written on both sides with His plan for history. The plan is sealed completely, so that no one who is unworthy can see it. John weeps with disappointment to think that no one can reveal the Father's plan. Then Christ appears before the Almighty throne as the perfect sacrifice, filled with all power, wisdom, and the Spirit of God. The universe rejoices that Christ is worthy to unveil the Father's plan!

Try This: *Spectacle Sharing*

Ask students to think of a time when they experienced something so awesome it gave them goose bumps, so sad it made them cry, so strange they couldn't describe it, or a combination of all three! Have students try to describe the experience in a way that will make others understand something of what they felt. Ask, "How successful are you at communicating your experience? What makes it difficult? What makes it rewarding? Why might it be particularly difficult for John to describe heaven?" (Answers will vary; be sure to point out the limitation of earthly language that John probably faced as he tried to record what he had seen.)

What Do the Words Mean? Clues to Chapters 4–5 *(25 minutes)*

Distribute copies of Vocabulary Page 3. Read the following explanations of the terms and images John uses. Explanations for words can be found in the glossary. Have students look up Scripture references if time allows you to dig deeper or to see examples of similar terms or images.

You may wish to have students work together in small groups. Assign each group a number of words to study. After allowing time for groups to complete their study, have them report their findings to the whole group. Then have students read Revelation 4–5 again. What do you discover that is new to you?

door standing open in heaven (4:1). An opportunity for John to glimpse heaven and see the world as those in heaven do (Luke 13:23–25; Acts 14:27).

jasper . . . carnelian . . . emerald (4:3). God's glory is described in terms of the reflected beauty of precious stones because no one can bear to look at God's brilliance directly. The three stones are among those used to describe the foundations of the New Jerusalem, since paradise is built on God's glory (Revelation 21:19–20).

twenty-four elders (4:4). All believers may be represented by the 12 tribes of Israel in the Old Testament and the 12 apostles of the New Testament.

crowns of gold (4:4). Represent victory, righteousness, and eternal life given to all believers who persevere in faith (2 Timothy 4:7–8; James 1:12).

lightning . . . thunder (4:5). Display the power and majesty of God in judgment (Exodus 9:23) and in warning (Exodus 19:16–17). God's voice is described as sounding like thunder (John 12:29–32).

sea of glass, clear as crystal (4:6). An image of peace, beauty, and purity before God's throne; where the chaos, destruction, and evil of the world are stilled (Exodus 24:9–10; Ezekiel 1:22). In front of the Jerusalem temple a large basin of water for ritual washing was known as the Sea (1 Kings 7:23–26).

four living creatures (4:6). Angelic beings who guard the heavenly throne, do God's bidding, and continually worship Him; similarly described by Ezekiel (1:5–10) and called seraphs by Isaiah (6:1–3). Their four faces may represent the noblest, strongest, wisest, and swiftest of all creation. In Christian art, the four creatures often represent the four Gospel writers: Matthew, the lion, who emphasizes Jesus as the Lion of Judah. The ox represents Luke, who emphasizes Jesus as the humble servant of all. The man portrays Mark, who emphasizes Jesus as God made man. The eagle is the symbol for John, who emphasizes Jesus as overcoming the world and seeing into the deep things of God. The creatures' wings are described by Isaiah as covering their eyes and feet while flying, suggesting that they do not consider themselves worthy to be exposed to God.

covered with eyes (4:6). Able to see everywhere at once, nothing escapes their attention (Ezekiel 1:18).

scroll (5:1). God's plan for history. The writing on both sides of a scroll was unusual, since writing on the outside vertical fibers of a papyrus scroll was more difficult than on the inside horizontal fibers. The image may have reminded readers of the stone tablets inscribed on both sides with the covenant law (Exodus 32:15).

sealed with seven seals (5:1). Completely secure and private, as letters—and Jesus' tomb (Matthew 27:65–66)—were sealed with wax so that no unauthorized person could open them and see inside. Under Roman civil law a person's last will and testament was sealed with seven seals. We do the same today when we seal things inside envelopes or lock them away in safes (Esther 8:8; Isaiah 29:11; Daniel 6:17).

Lion of the tribe of Judah (5:5). Christ, the Messiah, predicted in Genesis 49:9–10, where Judah's descendants are given the right to rule "until He comes to whom it belongs and the obedience of the nations is His." Jesus' mother, Mary, and stepfather, Joseph, were both of the tribe of Judah (Isaiah 11:1, 10; Luke 2:4).

Root of David (5:5). Christ, the Messiah, predicted in Isaiah 11:1 and identified in Romans 15:12 as an offshoot of David's father, Jesse. Through Mary and Joseph Jesus was a branch of Jesse and David's family tree, but Jesus was also their root, having created their ancestors.

Lamb (5:6). Christ, the Messiah, represented as the perfect lamb, sacrificed for the sins of the world, as predicted in Isaiah 53:7 and identified in John 1:29; 1 Corinthians 5:7; 1 Peter 1:18–19.

seven horns (5:6). Complete power and strength (Deuteronomy 33:17).

seven eyes (5:6). Complete intelligence and insight, the ability to see everything (Proverbs 15:3).

harp (5:8). A stringed instrument used to accompany the singing at God's throne (Revelation 14:2; 15:2–3).

incense (5:8). The prayers of the saints (Psalm 141:2).

new song (5:9). Praises sung by the redeemed, celebrating a new act of deliverance and blessing by God (Psalm 33:3; 96:1; 98:1; 144:9; Isaiah 42:10; Revelation 14:3).

Try This: *Site Seeing*

Have students create a collage or sketch of the throne room in heaven using the supplies provided. Encourage students to use the materials to cut out and paste together drawings, magazine photos, clip art, or construction-paper symbols to represent the various creatures and objects described by John. Use arrows to identify objects depicted and write brief explanations of what each object represents. Ask, "How does John's vision compare to the way heaven is pictured in movies, on television, and in advertising? What does the media usually leave out? Why?" (Answers will vary.)

Where's God When We Need Him? *(15 minutes)*

Ask students to share examples of times when they have felt that the world was "out of control." Reread Revelation 5, and ask, "When the world seems to be against you, what difference does it make to know that 'the Lamb is on the throne,' that Christ Jesus, who died for you, is ultimately in control of the universe?"

John's early Christian readers must have wondered, "Can't God see what we're going through? Why doesn't He do something about the pain, persecution, poverty, and other problems we're experiencing?" In answer, John is given a vision of the great throne in heaven, where God is surrounded by four living creatures with eyes to see everything that happens on earth. The sea, normally an image of chaos, is like glass—completely at peace before God's throne. God holds the plan for human history in His hand, and Christ Jesus alone is able to reveal it; because of His sacrifice on the cross, He has turned the tragedy of human history into a triumph.

The four living creatures keep repeating, "Holy, holy, holy is the Lord God Almighty, who was, and is, and is to come" (4:8). We sometimes think of God's holiness as bad news, since it means that God can't tolerate our sins. Yet at the same time, God's holiness also reveals something unknown to us that He will provide perfectly for those forgiven through faith in Christ. The creatures are witnesses that God is without fault in the past, present, and future. Their cry reminds us that God will make history turn out for good in the future, just as He has in the past. " 'For I know the plans I have for you,' declares the Lord, 'plans to prosper you and not to harm you, plans to give you hope and a future' " (Jeremiah 29:11).

The 24 elders respond, "You are worthy, our Lord and God" (4:11). The Roman Emperor Domitian had people chant these words when he made his entrance. But the glory of God in heaven makes the glory of any human king insignificant by comparison. Those who continue to worship the true God, even if it means persecution, will be rewarded. Recognizing God's glory enables us to consider, as Paul did, "that our present sufferings are not worth comparing with the glory that will be revealed in us" (Romans 8:18).

The message is clear; when we feel all alone, under attack, and out of control, we can take comfort from knowing that Christ is on the throne. God is in control, sees what we are going through, and has a perfect future planned. That future will be brought about by Christ Jesus, who died and rose again in order to reconcile us to God. We may have to suffer all kinds of troubles in this life, but we need never think that God has forgotten us or that He is punishing us. Jesus is worthy to receive everything good, because He gave everything He had to buy for us what we really need—forgiveness, freedom, God's favor, and a perfect future.

Try This: *Holy Help*

Provide paper and pens or pencils for students. Have students make a list of problems they are encountering: physical, social, emotional, financial, or

32

whatever. Ask them what kind of specialist could help them with each problem—a surgeon, mechanic, psychologist, banker? What kind of success rate in helping others would that professional need before they would trust that person—50 percent? 75? 90? Say, "Christ knows everything about you and has all the power necessary to help you deal with any problem. He is holy—His success rate is 100 percent. Paul writes in Philippians 4:13, 'I can do everything through Him who gives me strength.'" Ask students to spend some time in prayer asking the holy Lord who loves them and gave His life for them to also help them with the problems they listed. If your group is very comfortable with one another, you may want to have students swap lists and pray for one another.

Try This: *Songs of the Saints*

Instead of a closing prayer, consider ending this lesson by singing or listening to one of the many songs this portion of Scripture has inspired, such as "The Lamb," the Agnus Dei, "Holy, Holy, Holy," "Crown Him with Many Crowns," or one of the more contemporary songs that amplify and illustrate this vision of God's throne. Although we do not know the tune that accompanies the words found in Scripture, we can certainly join with all the saints in heaven and on earth by singing the praise of our Savior!

Closing *(2 minutes)*

Lord of heaven and earth, You see all our problems and pain. Enable us, through Your Holy Spirit, to see all Your greatness and glory, so that we can forget our worries and focus on Your worthiness. In Jesus Christ, our Redeemer, we pray. Amen.

door standing open in heaven **(4:1) Luke 13:23–25; Acts 14:27**

jasper . . . carnelian . . . emerald **(4:3) Revelation 21:19–20**

twenty-four elders **(4:4)**

crowns of gold **(4:4) 2 Timothy 4:7–8; James 1:12**

lightning . . . thunder **(4:5) Exodus 9:23; 19:16–17; John 12:29–32**

sea of glass, clear as crystal **(4:6) Exodus 24:9–10; Ezekiel 1:22; 1 Kings 7:23–26**

four living creatures **(4:6) Ezekiel 1:5–10; Isaiah 6:1–3**

covered with eyes **(4:6) Ezekiel 1:18**

scroll **(5:1) Exodus 32:15**

sealed with seven seals **(5:1) Matthew 27:65–66; Esther 8:8; Isaiah 29:11; Daniel 6:17**

Lion of the tribe of Judah **(5:5) Genesis 49:9–10; Isaiah 11:1, 10; Luke 2:4**

Root of David **(5:5) Isaiah 11:1; Romans 15:12**

Lamb **(5:6) Isaiah 53:7; John 1:29; 1 Corinthians 5:7; 1 Peter 1:18–19**

seven horns **(5:6) Deuteronomy 33:17**

seven eyes **(5:6) Proverbs 15:3**

harp **(5:8) Revelation 14:2; 15:2–3**

incense **(5:8) Psalm 141:2**

new song **(5:9) Psalm 33:3; 96:1; 98:1; 144:9; Isaiah 42:10; Revelation 14:3**

Activity	Suggested Time	Materials Needed
Opening	2 minutes	None
What Future Does Revelation Forecast? 　**Try This:** *Dream Definition*	15 minutes	None None
What Will Believers Endure? 　**Try This:** *Cycle Comparison*	20 minutes	None Bibles, Copies of Student Page 4
What Do the Words Mean? 　Clues to Chapters 6–16 　**Try This:** *Disaster Discussion*	optional activity	Copies of Vocabulary Page 4, Bibles None
How Will We Hold Up? 　**Try This:** *Security Seals*	15 minutes	None $5 bill, diploma, check, credit card, or other objects as suggested
Closing	2 minutes	None

REVELATION 6–16

Forecasting the Future—
What Will Believers Endure?

Purpose

Through the study of God's Word in Revelation, young people seek to identify the patterns of events and God's promises of protection in four visions of history revealed by Christ.

Opening *(2 minutes)*

God of the universe, thank You for Your presence in our lives. Send Your Holy Spirit to reassure us of Your control and enable us to worship You even when our world is falling apart. We pray through Jesus Christ, our victorious Savior. Amen.

What Future Does Revelation Forecast? *(15 minutes)*

In the preceding chapters of Revelation, Christ has directly addressed the churches and given John a glimpse of heaven to assure him and the reader that God is in control of history. Through John, Christ begins to reveal what all people will endure before the world ends. The main body of this revelation consists of four cycles of events, each leading up to God's judgment.

Three of the cycles are easily outlined as a series of seven events each: a scroll with seven seals broken open (6:1–8:5), seven warning trumpets blown (8:6–11:19), and seven bowls of judgment poured out (15:1–16:21). The third cycle, a vision of warfare in heaven (12:1–14:20), can also be grouped into seven events. This vision introduces figures (studied in the chapters that follow) to describe what will happen after Judgment Day. In each set of seven, God reassures or blesses His people during an interlude between the sixth and seventh events.

A common mistake in studying these sections of Scripture is to read them as a linear sequence of events: seven seals, followed by seven trumpets, followed by warfare in heaven, followed by seven plagues of judgment. Although the visions do flow one into the next, their organization in sets of seven and their common conclusion with God's judgment are clues that each set is complete in and of itself. Each vision has a different way of telling the same story. Such repetition is common in Scripture, even when God reveals the future: check out the two dreams given to Joseph in Genesis 37:5–10 or to Pharaoh in Genesis 41:17–32.

The four visions are clearly cycles, each describing the same events in a different way—but which events? There are four basic approaches to interpreting the predictions of Revelation, based on four different assumptions as to which events are being forecast:

Preterists assume that the visions all describe events that have already taken place—during the Roman persecution of first-century Christians and the decline of Rome that followed.

Futurists assume that the visions all describe events that have not yet happened—though persecutions and disasters during the Roman Empire gave a preview of struggles to come at the end of the world.

Historicists assume that the visions describe various events in church history from Christ's first coming to His return—some fulfilled in the days of Rome and others still to come in the future.

Idealists assume that the visions don't deal with actual events but are symbolic portrayals of the timeless struggle between good and evil—represented by the church (good) and Rome (evil).

Christ Himself describes the revelation as concerning "what is now and what will take place later" (Revelation 1:19). Therefore the historicists' view seems to best reflect His intention, recognizing that past and future, actual and symbolic fulfillment can all overlap. Many prophecies concerning Christ's first coming had both present and future meanings, so it seems likely that prophecies concerning His return will be similar. The events described in Revelation are intended to encourage all believers—since the time of John until the Last Day—to trust in Christ, resist false teachers, spread the faith, and be prepared, no matter what may happen before His return.

Try This: *Dream Definition*

Say, "Sleep experts say that the elements of our dreams can usually be found

in the things we were doing or thinking about in the two or three hours before we go to bed. Psychics argue that the elements of our dreams can be interpreted to tell us about the future. Freudian psychoanalysts contend that the elements of our dreams can be interpreted symbolically to tell us about our inner desires. What do you think?" Ask students to try to recall a vivid and lengthy dream that they have had recently. Have students take turns sharing and interpreting their dreams in small groups. Ask students to consider what might have produced the dream. What might it tell them about the future? (Most likely little or nothing.) About their subconscious mind? (It may tell them about bits of information that their brain has stored away.) How can different assumptions about what the dream refers to result in very different interpretations? (The approach will vary depending on the bias of the person.) How are these approaches to dream interpretation similar to the ways of interpreting Revelation? (The interpretation will vary depending on whether the reader sees Revelation as a view of the future, an image-driven process, or a literal interpretation.) Although interpreting Revelation may be difficult and challenging, the rest of God's Word guides our interpretive process and our conclusions.

What Will Believers Endure? *(20 minutes)*

A quick comparison of the four visions in chapters 6–16 reveal how similar the cycles are—especially the three announced as seven events each (visions 1, 2, 4). These three are also similar in how they view the end times and which events they include. All three begin with four man-made or natural disasters, emphasize warfare on earth, end in judgment, and view the world in terms of what believers will have to endure. By contrast, the unique cycle between the second and fourth cycles (12:1–14:20) begins with supernatural signs in heaven, emphasizes spiritual warfare, and ends in judgment, but views the world in terms of what God will do to defeat His enemies. Since this vision has a different focus, we will consider it in detail in Lesson 5.

The first four of the seven seals are announced by angels and call out afflictions that God allows to trouble the whole earth. They are represented by four messengers on colored horses, sometimes called "the four horsemen of the apocalypse." These four riders represent man-made disasters that result from human sin: conquest and dominance, war and violence, hunger and scarcity, death and the grave. A similar image is used in Zechariah 6:2–5, where chariots drawn by red, black, white, and dappled horses represent four spirits sent from heaven out across the earth as agents of divine judgment. In apocalyptic literature, common images such as horses seem to represent natural events, in contrast to strange images such as a dragon, which represent the supernatural. Jesus clearly predicts these natural afflictions in Matthew 24:4–13, where He warns that deceivers, wars and political turmoil, famines and earthquakes, persecutions and death will all trouble believers long before the end.

Some who interpret Revelation as a preview of an earthly millennial (thousand-year-long) rule of Christ on earth have argued that the first rider is Christ, since white usually means purity and crowns represent victory. After all, Jesus is depicted in Revelation 19:11 as riding a white horse while conquering. However, this first rider holds a battle bow, indicating victory through military means, and is presented as an equal with three others who represent war, hunger, and death. He is not clearly identified as Christ. In contrast, Jesus is clearly identified and supernaturally described in Revelation 19:11–15. There, He is depicted as wearing many crowns, conquering through His own blood, judging with the sword of God's Word, and being followed by the armies of heaven.

Others have suggested that the white rider is the antichrist, a specific person who appears like Christ but deceives and conquers the world. However, in Revelation 17–18 the prostitute (antichrist) attacks through seduction, not conquest, and wears no crown. **The best interpretation** is that the white horse and rider represent all kinds of conquest in general, especially whenever it brings disaster disguised as salvation.

The last three seals reveal a divine perspective on the events of human history. The fifth seal shows the martyrs in heaven, those who died for their Christian faith, calling on God to judge the earth and avenge their deaths. They are covered by the righteousness of Christ, but must wait for Judgment Day when God's plan will be completed. The sixth seal reveals the destruction of the heavens and the earth. An angel assures John this will not happen until all the servants of God have been sealed and saved by Christ. The opening of the seventh seal results in a dramatic pause, as all heaven anticipates the final judgment. God's angel throws an incense burner filled with prayers down to earth, signifying God's final judgment in response to the prayers of His people for justice and deliverance.

The seven trumpets announce a similar set of events. The first four are natural occurrences, similar to the plagues God imposed to free His people enslaved in Egypt. These plagues only afflict part of the world. An eagle warns that the last three will be much worse, and they are. The fifth trumpet announces the release of demons from the abyss of hell, who torment unbelievers. The sixth trumpet releases God's judgment in the form of massive, demon-inspired warfare, which results in a horrible death toll but does not persuade unbelievers to repent. Another mighty angel assures John that before the end, God's plan will be accomplished. The angel then commissions John to spread the message throughout the earth. The promise is so sure that John can measure the dimensions of the heaven, which awaits believers. He can also see the resurrection and vindication of the two witnesses who spread the Good News on earth. The seventh trumpet unleashes a great song of praise as God's judgment results in a return of His reign on earth as in heaven and brings reward for His faithful people.

Seven bowls of wrath are poured out in the fourth vision of history. The reader is assured that the things that plague people on earth come from God's tabernacle, where He keeps His promises to His people. The first four bowls are again natural disasters. Though the bowls clearly point to the end, unbelievers refuse to turn to God. The fifth bowl pours darkness on the throne of God's enemy, taking away his power to appear enlightened. The sixth bowl evaporates boundaries and releases demonic deceivers to gather all nations for the final battle. Before the end God Himself blesses those who are prepared and covered with Christ's righteousness. The seventh bowl brings the destruction of the earth and God's judgment on all His enemies.

Try This: *Cycle Comparison*

Have students skim Revelation 6–16 and fill in the outline found on Student Page 4. If you have a large group, you may wish to divide up the sections to be studied. Encourage students to write down what is described in the seven sections of each vision and what God says to His people in the interlude in each vision. Compare the four visions. How does each cycle differ in the events described? (See the notes in the lesson.) **How are they similar in the resulting judgment?** (All end with the judgment of humankind.)

The First Vision of History: Seven Seals Broken (6:1–8:5)

      1. Conquest and Dominance (6:1–2)

      2. War and Violence (6:3–4)

      3. Hunger and Scarcity (6:5–6)

      4. Death and the Grave (6:7–8)

      5. Persecution of the Saints (6:9–11)

      6. Destruction of the World (6:12–17)

      Interlude (7:1–17) Believers are sealed and saved by God

      7. Final Judgment (8:1–5)

The Second Vision of History: Seven Trumpets Blown (8:6–11:19)

1. Vegetation Burned (8:6–7)

2. Seas Destroyed (8:8–9)

3. Springs Poisoned (8:10–11)

4. Sky Darkened (8:12)

Interlude (8:13) An Eagle Cries Woe!

5. Demons Attack (9:1–12)

6. The World Is at War (9:13–21)

Interlude (10:1–11:14) Witnesses are sent and rescued by God

7. Final Judgment (11:15–19)

The Third Vision of History: Warfare in Heaven (12:1–14:20)

1. The Woman (12:1–2) A great and wondrous sign

2. The Dragon (12:3–4) Another sign

3. The Child (12:5–6)

4. The War (12:7–17)

5. The Two Beasts (13:1–18)

6. The Lamb and the 144,000 (14:1–5)

Interlude (14:6–13) Angels warn the world to worship God

7. The Harvest of the Earth (14:14–20)

The Fourth Vision of History: Seven Bowls Poured Out (15:1–16:21)

Introduction: Heaven Rejoices (15:1–8) Another great and marvelous sign

1. Disease Spread (16:1–2)

2. Seas Destroyed (16:3)

3. Springs Poisoned (16:4)

Interlude (16:5–7) The announcement that God's judgments are appropriate

4. Sun Scorches (16:8–9)

5. Evil Darkens (16:10–11)

6. Demons Wage War (16:12–14)

Interlude (16:15) Those ready and redeemed are blessed by God

7. Final Judgment (16:16–21)

What Do the Words Mean? Clues to Chapters 6–16 (optional activity)

Have students work through the following explanations of the terms and images John uses. Provide copies of Vocabulary Page 4 for students to record their findings. Explanations for words are in the glossary. Terms in chapters 12–14 are discussed in Lesson 5. If time allows, encourage students to look up the Scripture references in order to dig deeper or see examples of similar terms or images. You may want to assign groups to read Revelation 6–11 and 15–16 again. What kind of picture do you get from all the vivid symbolism?

white horse and rider (6:2). Human conquest, appearing as a savior but resulting in oppression.

red horse and rider (6:4). War and bloodshed, inflicting the sword of judgment on humanity.

black horse and rider (6:5). Scarcity as food production is disrupted and trade is imbalanced.

pale horse and rider (6:8). Death followed by the grave, afflicting a quarter of humanity at any given time by such means as violence, famine, plague, and animal attacks—the result of unchecked sinfulness.

white robe (6:11). Victory and purity through Christ's sacrifice (Revelation 7:9, 14).

earthquake (6:12). The end of the world on the Judgment Day of the Lord, described also in Ezekiel 38:19; Joel 2:31; 3:14–16; Isaiah 13:9; Haggai 2:6; Matthew 24:29; Mark 13:24–25.

wrath of the Lamb (6:16). Not the personal anger of God, but the reaction of His holiness against sin; God's rejection of those who reject Christ.

seal on the foreheads (7:3). Just as documents were sealed with wax, so all believers are identified and made secure to protect them in the judgment through God's recognition (Ephesians 4:30; 2 Timothy 2:19).

144,000 (7:4). The number of absolute completion (10 x 10 x 10) multiplied by the number of God's people (12 x 12); clearly identified in Revelation 14:3 as all those "who had been redeemed from the earth." This is not literally Israel or even Jewish believers; note that the tribe of Manasseh, one of Joseph's sons, is included with Joseph, while the tribe of Dan (Genesis 49:1–28) is omitted, perhaps due to an association with idolatry (Judges 18:30).

multitude (7:9). Believers of all nations and languages stand before God because they remained faithful and are washed clean by Christ's sacrifice (Revelation 7:14).

palm branches (7:9). An ancient symbol of joy and victory (Leviticus 23:40; John 12:13).

great tribulation (7:14). Troubles and persecutions of believers, especially leading up to the end of the world (Daniel 12:1; Mark 13:19).

silence in heaven (8:1). A dramatic pause that builds anticipation and emphasizes the importance of what is to follow, as when people quiet down before a play or movie is about to begin.

censer (8:3). A container of burning coals used to burn incense, representing the storing of prayers (Revelation 8:5).

hurled it on the earth (8:5). The casting of the censer to earth, with thunder, lightning, and an earthquake. This event connects God's judgments on the earth with the prayers of His people for justice.

trumpets (8:6). Loud instruments used to announce important events, sound warnings, and send signals during times of war (Numbers 10:9).

Wormwood (8:11). A bitter plant, representing sorrow and disaster.

eagle (8:13). A sharp-sighted messenger of God, flying above the first four disasters (Isaiah 40:31).

Woe! (8:13). A prophetic warning of disaster that will cause grief (Matthew 23:13–29).

star that had fallen (9:1). Satan. Stars represent angels in Revelation 1:20 and in Jewish tradition. Satan is a fallen angel, inhabiting the Abyss of hell and leading the demons.

Abyss (9:1). Hell, the place of the demons, represented by an almost bottomless pit (Luke 8:31).

locusts (9:3). Demons, represented by the terrible plague of insects that could cover a land and destroy all food (Joel 1:1–2:11). Instead of consuming vegetation, these locusts are given power to sting unbelievers.

five months (9:5). A temporary period, perhaps modeled on the life cycle of locusts (Revelation 9:10).

like crowns of gold (9:7). The appearance, but not the reality, of victory.

human faces (9:7). Having human intelligence and cunning.

women's hair (9:8). Having human beauty and attractiveness.

lions' teeth (9:8). Ferocity and savagery in attack (Joel 1:6).

breastplates of iron (9:9). Armor to protect from counterattack.

sound of . . . battle (9:9). Power to create fear even before striking.

tails and stings like scorpions (9:10). Inflicting severe pain; not necessarily fatal.

Abaddon and Apollyon (9:11). Both mean "destroyer," describing Satan's purpose.

horns of the golden altar (9:13). Projections resembling animal horns at the corners of the temple altars where those fleeing judgment could find mercy (1 Kings 1:50–51).

four angels who are bound (9:14). Agents of God's judgment, held back until the end of the world, when they will release the power of a massive war in a final attempt to turn unbelievers left on earth back to God.

Euphrates (9:14). The longest river in western Asia, often marking the boundary between Israel and enemies to the east; perhaps represents a point from the beginning of the earth (Genesis 2:14).

two hundred million troops (9:16). A huge, nonspecific number of demons, "twenty thousands times ten thousands" in Greek, twice the "ten thousand times ten thousand" found elsewhere in Scripture (Daniel 7:10; Revelation 5:11).

horses and riders (9:17). Like the cavalry, a fast-moving and unstoppable army.

fiery red, dark blue, and yellow as sulfur (9:17). May refer to colors worn by Roman troops, or may indicate the riders' authority as the fire and sulfur of God's judgment.

heads of lions (9:17). Images of ferocity and savagery in attacking and killing.

fire, smoke and sulfur that came out of their mouths (9:18). Authority to produce devastation, death, and destruction as a sign of God's wrath.

tails were like snakes (9:19). Demonic power to injure those who escape being killed in a frontal attack.

robed in a cloud (10:1). Concealed by the same means God used to reveal His glory (Exodus 13:21; 14:19–20; 24:15–18; 40:34–35; Numbers 9:15–23; Deuteronomy 31:15–16; Matthew 24:30; Mark 13:26; Luke 21:27).

rainbow (10:1). Sign of God's promise to never again destroy the earth by flood (Genesis 9:15–16; Ezekiel 1:28).

legs . . . like fiery pillars (10:1). A reminder of God's presence and protection in dark times, like the cloud and pillar of fire that led Israel in the desert (Exodus 13:21).

little scroll (10:2). A limited revelation, but seen by the whole world (Revelation 10:9–10).

right foot on the sea . . . left foot on the land (10:2). Having power over the whole world (Genesis 1:10; Psalm 95:5; Jonah 1:9; Revelation 7:1–2).

like the roar of a lion (10:3). Loud, authoritative, threatening (Proverbs 19:12; 20:2).

seven thunders (10:3). The sound of absolute divine judgment (Revelation 8:5; 11:19; 16:18).

seal up (10:4). Delay speaking until the time is right (Daniel 8:26).

take it and eat it (10:9). Grasp and fully digest (comprehend) the contents (Ezekiel 3:1–3).

sweet as honey (10:10). The message will bring delight (Ezekiel 3:1–3).

stomach turned sour (10:10). The content of the message will bring pain (Job 20:12–14).

measure the temple (11:1). God's promise to rebuild His relationship with humanity and restore perfect worship is so certain it already can be described in detail and literally counted on (Ezekiel 40:2–5; Zechariah 2:1–5).

exclude the outer court (11:2). Just as Gentiles could occupy the outer court of the Temple, so pagan nations will be allowed to persecute God's people on the outside—though true, inner worship will be preserved.

trample on the holy city (11:2). God's people, as the city of Jerusalem, will be abused for a time.

42 months (11:2). A time of evil and brokenness; 1,260 days in the Jewish lunar calendar; the period of time the two witnesses prophesy in 11:3 and the woman (church) is protected while being pursued by the dragon (Satan) in 12:6. It also equals "a time, times and half a time" (3½ years), during which God will protect the woman (church) in Revelation 12:14. Since these numbers all have the same value and refer to related events, they are best understood to be the same time period referred to in different ways, a technique used often in apocalypses (Daniel 12:7).

two witnesses (11:3). The testimony of God's people personified by two individuals, probably Moses and Elijah, who represented the Law and Prophets as witnesses to Jesus' transfiguration (Matthew 17:2–3). According to Jewish law, truth was established by the testimony of two witnesses (Deuteronomy 19:15), so Jesus urged acceptance of His message (John 8:16–18) and sent disciples out in teams of two (Mark 6:7; Luke 10:1; Acts 13:2; 15:39–40). Some also see the two witnesses as representing the Old and New Covenants (Hebrews 12:18–24), the prophets and the apostles (Ephesians 2:19–20), or the messages of Law and Gospel (Romans 8:1–4).

two olive trees; two lampstands (11:4). The two witnesses are described as two olive trees, sources of oil for anointing and light, and two lampstands, which generally represent the people of God (Revelation 1:20). Similar images are used in Zechariah 4:1–14, where a lampstand with seven lights represent Israel and two olive trees are described as "the two who are anointed to serve the Lord of all the earth" (verse 14).

fire . . . from their mouths (11:5). God gives His two witnesses the power to call down God's judgment and consuming wrath (2 Samuel 22:9; Jeremiah 5:14).

power to shut up the sky . . . to turn the waters into blood (11:6). Drought and poisoned water, the same signs of God's wrath that accompanied the messages of Elijah (1 Kings 17:1) and Moses (Exodus 7:17–21).

beast . . . from the Abyss (11:7). The force of Satan, the angel of the Abyss (Revelation 9:11).

bodies will lie in the street (11:8). People will refuse to show any respect, even in death. To refuse a person burial is an ultimate insult in the Middle East.

great city . . . where also their Lord was crucified (11:8). Literally Jerusalem or figuratively the church, depicted here as immoral, idolatrous, and persecuting the righteous.

Sodom (11:8). A notorious place of immorality destroyed by God through fire (Genesis 13:13; 19:1–25; Isaiah 3:8–9).

Egypt (11:8). The infamous place of Israel's slavery and a source of idolatry (Exodus 2:23; Ezekiel 20:7–8).

three and a half days (11:11). A short time of evil celebration, in proportion to the 3½ years the two witnesses preached to the world, but not long enough for the world to forget them.

breath of life from God (11:11). The resurrection of the witnesses of the church is accomplished through God's Spirit (Genesis 2:7; Ezekiel 37:5, 10).

up to heaven in a cloud (11:12). Just as Jesus is resurrected and taken up to heaven, so the faithful witnesses are glorified and taken home to God before the final judgment (Acts 1:9).

temple in heaven was opened (11:19). God reveals His holy presence to all people and welcomes believers through the work of Christ on the cross (Luke 23:44–46).

ark of His covenant (11:19). A symbol of God's presence and faithfulness to His people, the ark held God's law and traveled with His people Israel (Numbers 10:33–36).

sea of glass mixed with fire (15:2). Peaceful calm (the experience of believers) mixed with the fire of judgment (the experience of unbelievers) before God's throne (Revelation 4:6).

song of Moses (15:3). Not literally what Moses sang after God freed Israel, but the same message: all nations know God alone is holy, glorious, and worthy of worship by the way He saves His people (Exodus 15:1–18).

song of the Lamb (15:3). Not what Jesus sang, but what is sung about Him: all nations know God alone is holy, glorious, and worthy of worship by the way He saves His people (Philippians 2:5–11).

tabernacle of the Testimony (15:5). The dwelling of God with His people while the Israelites wandered in the desert; this tent held the testimony of God's law (Exodus 38:21) and was replaced by Christ (Hebrews 9:11–14).

clean, shining linen (15:6). A covering of righteousness and glory (Revelation 19:8).

golden sashes (15:6). A sign of honor and dignity bestowed by a king (Exodus 28:40).

frogs (16:13). Demonic spirits misleading people to serve Satan, the political beast, and the false church, as frogs conjured by magicians misled Pharaoh (Exodus 8:2–7).

Armageddon (16:16)— Har Mageddon, literally translated as "the mountain of Megiddo," was a strategic location overlooking a famous battlefield and crossroads, one of the few places large armies could assemble in ancient Israel. Probably not the actual location, but a symbol of massive warfare against God (2 Chronicles 35:20–24).

hailstones (16:21). Another sign of God's final judgment, which cannot be escaped by running away from the cities (Exodus 9:23; Ezekiel 13:10–14).

Try This: *Disaster Discussion*

Ask students to think about the last disaster they experienced personally or saw on the news. Did they consider it a sign of God's judgment or just a result of living in a world broken by human sinfulness? (Answers may vary, but help students understand that disaster is a result of sin in the world.) **Do they think anyone will turn back to God as a result, or will people instead blame and curse God?** (Both reactions are common as a result of disaster.) **How are all the tragedies we experience part of our preparation for the end of the world?** (The disasters we experience now are a mere shadow of the final destruction of the earth. As believers in Christ, we have God's promise of an eternal rescue from the suffering unbelievers will endure.)

How Will We Hold Up? *(15 minutes)*

Each vision of history in this section of Revelation describes God's purpose behind a series of disasters and demonic attacks leading up to the end. Each vision has a message for believers. The first cycle, marked by the seven seals, assures those who died for their faith that God will avenge their deaths. The second cycle, announced by seven trumpets, calls all people to repent and urges believers to spread the message of salvation. The third cycle, describing the spiritual warfare behind the sufferings of the church, "calls for patient endurance on the part of the saints who obey God's commandments and remain faithful to Jesus" (Revelation 14:12). The fourth cycle, marked by the pouring out of seven plagues, does all three: assures martyrs of justice (16:5–6), calls all people to repentance (16:9–11), and urges believers to persevere (16:15).

Each of the cycles is interrupted by God's promise of protection from spiritual harm and reward for earthly sufferings. In the first cycle, an important break before the final judgment reveals that God will mark all believers with a seal to ensure their righteousness, victory, and perfect joy in paradise (Revelation 7:1–17). In the second cycle, a long pause in the same place commissions John to spread the message of God's judgment and paradise, then describes the ultimate victory of the two witnesses of the church (Revelation 10:1–11:14). In the third cycle, the same kind of interlude before the harvest of the earth reveals the spread of the eternal Gospel, warns of judgment on God's enemies, and pronounces a blessing on "the dead who die in the Lord" (Revelation 14:6–13). The fourth cycle begins with a reassuring vision of the believers singing God's praises in heaven, and then again, just before the end, blesses those who persevere and are prepared for Christ's return (16:15).

The overall message is clear: though history will be full of disasters and demonic attacks, those with faith in Christ will be rewarded in paradise and ultimately avenged by God for their sufferings on earth. In the meantime, the power of the Holy Spirit enables us to persevere in spreading the Good News of salvation through Christ's sacrifice and warning all people to repent of their sins before God's final judgment.

Try This: *Security Seals*

Gather and examine some of the following items: a $5 bill, a diploma, a check, a credit card, a new software program, an unopened bottle of pain reliever, or other "brand" name items. Ask students, "How do you know that these items are authentic and can be trusted?" (They are sealed or marked in some way.) **"What security seals or identifying marks can be checked to make sure they are the real deal?"** (Answers will vary.) **"What images does John use in Revelation to assure believers that God can be trusted, in spite of the disasters that will come upon us before the end?"** (The victorious lamb, promise of the angels, and others.)

Closing *(2 minutes)*

Living God, thank You for the justice that will come at the end of this world; the seal that You placed on us through Baptism, which spares us from the just and condemning sentence; the promises You give us in Your Word; and the paradise that awaits us in heaven. Give us power through Your Holy Spirit to persevere in spreading the good news of Your salvation and warning others of Your judgment. All this we pray through Jesus Christ, our Lord. Amen.

The First Vision of History: Seven Seals Broken **(6:1–8:5)**

    1. **(6:1–2)**

    2. **(6:3–4)**

    3. **(6:5–6)**

    4. **(6:7–8)**

    5. **(6:9–11)**

    6. **(6:12–17)**

    Interlude **(7:1–17)**

    7. **(8:1–5)**

The Second Vision of History: Seven Trumpets Blown **(8:6–11:19)**

    1. **(8:6–7)**

    2. **(8:8–9)**

    3. **(8:10–11)**

    4. **(8:12)**

    Interlude **(8:13)**

    5. **(9:1–12)**

    6. **(9:13–21)**

    Interlude **(10:1–11:14)**

    7. **(11:15–19)**

The Third Vision of History: Warfare in Heaven **(12:1–14:20)**

    1. **(12:1–2)**

    2. **(12:3–4)**

3. **(12:5–6)**

4. **(12:7–17)**

5. **(13:1–18)**

6. **(14:1–5)**

Interlude **(14:6–13)**

7. **(14:14–20)**

The Fourth Vision of History: Seven Bowls Poured Out **(15:1–16:21)**

Introduction: **(15:1–8)**

1. **(16:1–2)**

2. **(16:3)**

3. **(16:4)**

Interlude **(16:5–7)**

4. **(16:8–9)**

5. **(16:10–11)**

6. **(16:12–14)**

Interlude **(16:15)**

7. **(16:16–21)**

white horse and rider **(6:2)**

red horse and rider **(6:4)**

black horse and rider **(6:5)**

pale horse and rider **(6:8)**

white robe **(6:11) Revelation 7:9, 14**

earthquake **(6:12) Ezekiel 38:19; Joel 2:31; 3:14–16; Isaiah 13:9; Haggai 2:6; Matthew 24:29; Mark 13:24–25**

wrath of the Lamb **(6:16)**

seal on the foreheads **(7:3) Ephesians 4:30; 2 Timothy 2:19**

144,000 **(7:4) Genesis 49:1–28; Judges 18:30**

multitude **(7:9) Revelation 7:14**

palm branches **(7:9) Leviticus 23:40; John 12:13**

great tribulation **(7:14) Daniel 12:1; Mark 13:19**

silence in heaven **(8:1)**

censer **(8:3) Revelation 8:5**

hurled it on the earth **(8:5)**

trumpets **(8:6) Numbers 10:9**

Wormwood **(8:11)**

eagle **(8:13) Isaiah 40:31**

Woe! **(8:13) Matthew 23:13–29**

star that had fallen **(9:1)**

Abyss **(9:1) Luke 8:31**

locusts **(9:3) Joel 1:1–2:11**

five months **(9:5) Revelation 9:10**

like crowns of gold **(9:7)**

human faces **(9:7)**

women's hair **(9:8)**

lions' teeth **(9:8) Joel 1:6**

breastplates of iron **(9:9)**

sound of . . . battle **(9:9)**

tails and stings like scorpions **(9:10)**

Abaddon and Apollyon **(9:11)**

horns of the golden altar **(9:13) 1 Kings 1:50–51**

four angels who are bound **(9:14)**

Euphrates **(9:14) Genesis 2:14**

two hundred million troops **(9:16) Daniel 7:10; Revelation 5:11**

horses and riders **(9:17)**

fiery red, dark blue, yellow as sulfur **(9:17)**

heads of lions **(9:17)**

fire, smoke and sulfur that came out of their mouths **(9:18)**

tails were like snakes **(9:19)**

robed in a cloud **(10:1) Exodus 13:21; 14:19–20; 24:15–18; 40:34–35; Numbers 9:15–23; Deuteronomy 31:15–16; Matthew 24:30; Mark 13:26; Luke 21:27**

rainbow **(10:1) Genesis 9:15–16; Ezekiel 1:28**

legs . . . like fiery pillars **(10:1) Exodus 13:21**

little scroll **(10:2)**

right foot on the sea . . . left foot on the land **(10:2) Genesis 1:10; Psalm 95:5; Jonah 1:9; Revelation 7:1–2**

like the roar of a lion **(10:3) Proverbs 19:12; 20:20**

seven thunders **(10:3) Revelation 8:5; 11:19; 16:18**

seal up **(10:4) Daniel 8:26**

take it and eat it **(10:9) Ezekiel 3:1–3**

sweet as honey **(10:10) Ezekiel 3:1–3**

stomach turned sour **(10:10) Job 20:12–14**

measure the temple **(11:1) Ezekiel 40:2–5; Zechariah 2:1–5**

exclude the outer court **(11:2)**

trample on the holy city **(11:2)**

42 months **(11:2) Daniel 12:7**

two witnesses **(11:3) Matthew 17:2–3; Deuteronomy 19:15; John 8:16–18; Mark 6:7; Luke 10:1; Acts 13:2; 15:39–40; Hebrews 12:18–24; Ephesians 2:19–20; Romans 8:1–4**

two olive trees; two lampstands **(11:4) Revelation 1:20; Zechariah 4:1–14**

fire . . . from their mouths **(11:5) 2 Samuel 22:9; Jeremiah 5:14**

power to shut up the sky . . . to turn the waters into blood **(11:6) 1 Kings 17:1; Exodus 7:17–21**

beast . . . from the Abyss **(11:7) Revelation 9:11**

bodies will lie in the street **(11:8)**

great city . . . where also their Lord was crucified **(11:8)**

Sodom **(11:8) Genesis 13:13; 19:1–25; Isaiah 3:8–9**

Egypt **(11:8) Exodus 2:23; Ezekiel 20:7–8**

three and a half days **(11:11)**

breath of life from God **(11:11) Genesis 2:7; Ezekiel 37:5, 10** up to heaven in a cloud **(11:12) Acts 1:9**

temple in heaven was opened **(11:19) Luke 23:44–46**

ark of His covenant **(11:19) Numbers 10:33–36**

sea of glass mixed with fire **(15:2) Revelation 4:6**

song of Moses **(15:3) Exodus 15:1–18**

song of the Lamb **(15:3) Philippians 2:5–11**

tabernacle of the Testimony **(15:5) Exodus 38:21; Hebrews 9:11–14**

clean, shining linen **(15:6)**

golden sashes **(15:16) Exodus 28:40**

frogs **(16:13) Exodus 8:2–7**

Armageddon **(16:16) 2 Chronicles 35:20–24**

hailstones **(16:21) Exodus 9:23; Ezekiel 13:10–14**

5

Defeating the Devil—
Who Are the Dragon, the Beasts,
and the Prostitute?

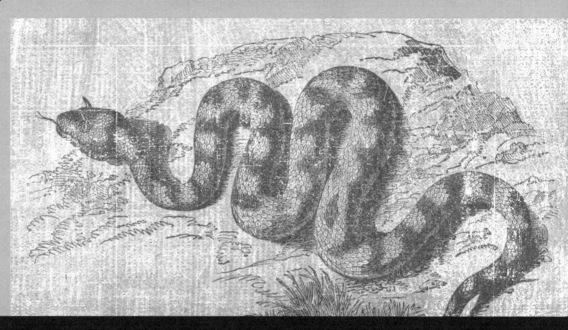

Purpose

Through the study of Revelation, the students will learn to recognize and, with the Holy Spirit's power, resist the agents of evil and persecution.

Lesson Outline 5

Activity	Suggested Time	Materials Needed
Opening	2 minutes	None
Who Is the Dragon? **Try This:** *Coverage Comparison*	15 minutes	None Video of newscast, newspaper, news magazine
Who Are the Beasts? **Try This:** *Nemesis Naming*	10 minutes	None Information on persecuted Christians
Who Is the Antichrist? **Try This:** *Script Scrutiny*	10 minutes	None Books/movies about the end times
What Is the Mark of the Beast? **Try This:** *Invisible Ink*	10 minutes	None Invisible ink or washable yellow marker
What Do the Words Mean? Clues to Chapters 12–14; 17–18	optional activity	Copies of Vocabulary Page 5, Bibles
How Is the Devil Defeated? **Try This:** *Spoil Sports*	10 minutes	None News article about sporting event
Closing	2 minutes	None

Opening (2 minutes)

Lord of Lords, just as You sent Your Son to save us from death and eternal damnation, send Your Spirit to protect us from the attacks of Satan, so that we may be ready to celebrate Your final victory. Through Jesus Christ, our Savior, we pray. Amen.

Who Is the Dragon? (15 minutes)

In chapters 6–16 four visions of history are revealed. Three consist of sets of seven events, including a great battle on earth, followed by judgment. The third set of events is a somewhat different vision. Since it is revealed along with the others and also ends with the judgment, it seems to reveal the same future. However, this vision is not clearly marked as a set of seven, it begins before the judgments are poured out, and it involves a great battle in both heaven and earth between a dragon and the offspring of a woman.

The identities of the dragon, the woman, and her offspring are no mystery. In fact, the third chapter of Genesis predicts these events. When God cursed the serpent who led Adam and Eve to disobey and fall into sin, God said, "I will put enmity between you and the woman, and between your offspring and hers; He will crush your head, and you will strike His heel" (Genesis 3:15). The dragon is clearly described in Revelation as "that ancient serpent called the devil, or Satan, who leads the whole world astray" (Revelation 12:9). The "woman clothed with the sun" (12:1) represents the church—all of Eve's descendants who are faithful to God and reflect Christ, the sun of righteousness (Malachi 4:2; see also Luke 1:78). Jesus was the unique offspring of Eve who crushed Satan's head and his power to accuse by being wounded and dying on the cross for the sins of all humanity. The rest of her offspring are described as "those who obey God's commandments and hold to the testimony of Jesus" (Revelation 12:17).

The appearance of the woman is a great and wondrous sign, since from God's faithful people Christ the Messiah was born. The appearance of the dragon is also a sign, but neither great nor wondrous. The dragon appears to have perfect authority (seven heads), complete power (ten horns), and is accompanied by a substantial number of fallen angels (stars swept to earth). Satan wants to destroy the Son of God, but Christ completes His mission and returns to God's throne. Satan and his angels are defeated by Michael and the angels of God, and they are cast out of heaven. Christ's salvation has replaced Satan's accusations before God's throne. Therefore, those who trust in the blood of Christ and the testimony of His victory overcome Satan, even when they are put to death for their faith. The church may undergo testing and trials, but just as the woman is protected in the desert, we cannot be destroyed by Satan.

Try This: Coverage Comparison

To help students better understand this activity, you may want to record a news story from a local or national television newscast. Provide students with newspaper or news magazine articles that cover the same story. Ask students to compare television news coverage of an event with coverage of the same event in a newspaper or magazine. **Which story is easier to understand?** (Various answers.) **Which gives more details?** (Most frequently the print account will provide more details.) **Which better explains why the event happened?** (Answers may vary.) **What is the advantage of seeing the story in several ways?** (We have different learning styles; the story is told from different perspectives.) **Have students consider the same questions as they compare the seven days of creation recorded in Genesis 1:1–2:3 with the story of creation in Genesis 2:4–25. Use the same questions to compare the seven-part series in Revelation 16 to the story in Revelation 12:1–14:20.** (Though the events are described differently, both accounts tell of God's triumph over the enemy.)

Who Are the Beasts? *(10 minutes)*

When Satan is unable to stop Christ or His church, he conjures two terrible beasts to attack individual believers. The first comes as an invader from the sea and has features of the leopard, bear, and lion. These violent predators call to mind the Greek, Persian, and Babylonian Empires in the vision of Daniel 7:4–6. The beast has 10 horns, like the fourth beast foreseen in Daniel 7:7, which represented the Roman Empire.

Several Roman emperors demanded that they be worshiped as gods, blasphemed the true God, and persecuted Christians who resisted them. The first beast is clearly modeled after the powerful Roman Empire, which dominated the known world in New Testament times. One of the 10 heads of the beast even recovers from a wound that seemed fatal, a detail which may have reminded early Christians of the Roman emperor Caligula (A.D. 37–41), who recovered after being thought terminally ill. Although the Roman Empire had tremendous power and may have seemed to conquer the saints, the Christian church ultimately outlasted it. In fact, when Emperor Constantine declared himself a Christian in A.D. 328, it seemed as though the saints conquered the Romans! The description of the first beast as having authority over every tribe, people, language, and nation (13:7) suggests that it represents not only Roman rule, but every political empire that persecutes God's people, coming back to life in various powerful governments and institutions, from the time of Christ to the end of the world.

The second beast comes from the earth, from among the very people it attacks. The fact that it has the horns of a lamb implies that it has the power of a religious institution and even the appearance of Christ. But this beast actually speaks on behalf of the dragon. It deceives people through false miracles and enforces worship of the political beast, especially the head that seemed fatally wounded. The second beast also controls trade, so that only those marked as belonging to the political beast can buy or sell.

In John's day, the second beast certainly resembled the pagan religious establishment, which supported worship of the Roman Emperors as part of a system of many gods. The pagan priests were able to simulate miracles and often instigated persecution of Christians. Since much of the meat and produce sold in markets was first offered to idols, it was difficult for Christians to buy and sell without supporting the worship of false gods. The mark of this beast might even be a reflection of pagan religious tattoos, by which people showed their loyalty to a particular idol. However, this beast is also described as ruling over the entire earth and therefore could represent false religion in general, which deceives people and leads them into false worship. It may also be any institution that claims to represent God but actually speaks for Satan.

Try This: *Nemesis Naming*

A *nemesis* is an enemy that comes back repeatedly to attack or challenge someone. It is estimated that more Christians have been tortured or killed for their faith in the last hundred years than in any previous century in the history of the church. How many governments can students name that have repeatedly attacked or challenged Christians? (Answers will vary depending on student knowledge.) Which governments may be acting as the first beast today, persecuting and executing Christians? (These might include Somalia, China, fundamentalist Islamic nations, and others around the globe.) Which false religions have attacked Christians, often with government support? (Predominantly Muslim extremists at this time. While not technically a religion, Communism has also attempted to suppress the Christian church.) Students may want to learn more about the work of the beasts today by reading *The Narrow Road: Stories of Those Who Walk This Road Together* by Brother Andrew, with John and Elizabeth Sherrill (© 2001 Revell Books). This book contains stories of modern-day persecuted Christians, including those living in Sudan, China, and fundamentalist Islamic nations. Another good resource is *Jesus Freaks: DC Talk and the Voice of the Martyrs—Stories of Those Who Stood for*

Jesus, the Ultimate Jesus Freaks (© 1999 Albury Publishing). Information is also available by searching under "persecuted Christians" on the Internet.

Who Is the Antichrist? *(10 minutes)*

The specific identity of the second beast and the meaning of its number are among the most perplexing questions raised by Revelation. Since John gives a number equivalent to the name of the beast and calls it "man's number" (13:18), many assume John had a specific person in mind. Representing names of individuals by their numeric equivalents, a practice known as *gematria*, was a popular way to avoid getting in trouble for "naming names" in John's day. However, since the same number could represent many different names, messages using such numbers could only be understood if the reader already knew who the number might represent. Some think 666 might represent the tyrant Nero Caesar, a name that in Hebrew characters could add up to 666. But John was writing in Greek and Nero had been dead 20 years when Revelation was written. Possible Greek equivalents could be Euanthas, Lateinos, or Domitian, who was the ruling emperor when John had his vision. But which one John is referring to, if any, remains unclear. Those who interpret Revelation as future-focused often equate the religious beast with the antichrist, which John warned of in his first two letters. This viewpoint has been the focus of several movie plots and many popular books. All of these movies and books warn of a world figure to come who will try to exterminate Christians with the backing of a united world government.

However, there is no agreement as to whom exactly John had in mind, or whether he was even thinking of a particular person. While 666 may be "man's number" in the sense that it identifies a person acting as the anti-Christian religious beast, it may also be "man's number" in the general sense of evil and imperfect humanity trying to take the place of God. Symbolically, 666 may represent the unholy trinity of three evils (Satan, political oppression, and religious deception) posing as the Holy Trinity. Such a coalition has brought persecution to Christians repeatedly throughout world history. If the religious beast is equivalent to the antichrist mentioned in John's letters, then it certainly refers to a repeated trend in history, rather than a specific, future person. John says that "as you have heard that the antichrist is coming, even now many antichrists have come" (1 John 2:18). "Who is the liar? It is the man who denies that Jesus is the Christ. Such a man is the antichrist" (1 John 2:22). "Every spirit that does not acknowledge Jesus is not from God. This is the spirit of the antichrist, which you have heard is coming and even now is already in the world" (1 John 4:3). "Deceivers, who do not acknowledge Jesus Christ as coming in the flesh, have gone out into the world. Any such person is the deceiver and the antichrist" (2 John 1:7).

Try This: *Script Scrutiny*

Encourage students to recall books or movies featuring the antichrist as an individual or institution pretending to represent God but actually working to wipe out Christians. How realistic is the story line? (Very far-fetched.) **How well supported is the plot from the clear passages of Scripture?** (The plots are often loosely based on Scripture, if at all.) **What point are the authors or directors trying to make?** (The "agenda" of most is unclear, usually fear or an excuse for gore.) **Do you think such speculation is helpful or harmful to the Christian cause?** (Frequently it is harmful, since Christians are often portrayed as stupid or foolish.)

What Is the Mark of the Beast? *(10 minutes)*

Controversy surrounds not only the identity of the beast but the nature of its mark. Those who view Revelation as speaking primarily to the first century see the mark as a reference to pagan religious tattoos. Those who view Revelation as entirely literal and future-focused warn against identity marks, such as bar codes, microchips, or Social Security numbers, which may be required by a future, anti-

Christian world government. (Make sure that students understand that this is not an official teaching of our church.) Revelation itself contrasts the mark of the beast with the seal placed on the foreheads of the servants of God to identify and protect them (Revelation 7:3; 9:4). Paul describes the seal of God as the confession of the true faith (2 Timothy 2:19) and the presence of the Holy Spirit (Ephesians 4:30) rather than a visible, physical mark. In the same way, the mark of the beast may be understood as an indication of a false faith and the presence of an evil spirit. In any event, it is not the mark in itself that condemns people, but their worship of the beast and its image rather than the true God (Revelation 14:9–10; 16:2; 19:20). Whether the mark is literal or not, those who trust in Christ need not worry, because "there is now no condemnation for those who are in Christ Jesus" (Romans 8:1).

Try This: *Invisible Ink*

Use invisible ink or a washable yellow marker to draw the name or a symbol of Christ on your students' right hand or forehead. Ask, "How does it feel to know that God can see those who belong to Him at all times?" (Exciting or scary.) **"How does it feel to know that many people have already allowed themselves to be marked as belonging to the beast?"** (Knowing that so many have turned away from God saddens many believers.) **"How would life be different if everyone could see who belongs to whom at all times?"** (Answers will vary.) **"How important is it that God sees and judges the heart, not the outward appearance (1 Samuel 16:7)?"** (This is critical. No one will be able to fool God. He knows His own.) **"How is Baptism like a seal marking us as belonging to Christ Jesus?"** (While not a visible mark, it, too, is a seal on our lives as one marked with the cross of Christ. Baptism sets us apart as God's chosen child.)

What Do the Words Mean? Clues to Chapters 12–15; 17–20 *(optional activity)*

Distribute copies of Vocabulary Page 5. Allow students to work in small groups. Assign each group a number of terms to research and report back about. Review the following explanations of what the terms and images John uses may mean. Explanations for words are in the glossary. Students should look up the Scripture references if they want to dig deeper or see examples of similar terms or images found elsewhere in Scripture. Then read chapters 12–14 and 17–18 of Revelation. Which images are the most difficult to understand?

> *woman clothed with the sun* (12:1). God's faithful people, the church, reflecting the radiance of Christ (Luke 1:78–79) as His bride (Isaiah 54:1; 62:5; Jeremiah 2:2; Ephesians 5:25; 2 Corinthians 11:2).

> *moon under her feet* (12:1). Authority over any lesser power, as the moon is less than the sun (Genesis 37:9; 1 Corinthians 15:41; Isaiah 30:26). Being under a foot implies submission (1 Kings 5:3; Psalm 8:6; 47:3; Matthew 22:44; Ephesians 1:22; Hebrews 2:7–8).

> *crown of twelve stars* (12:1). A crown of victory (2 Timothy 2:5), or angels who fight for all the churches (Revelation 1:20).

> *red dragon* (12:3). "That ancient serpent called the devil, or Satan, who leads the whole world astray" (Revelation 12:9).

> *seven heads* (12:3). Perfect authority, or perhaps seven (imperfect) Roman emperors (Revelation 13:1; 17:3).

> *ten horns* (12:3). Complete power, dominating all other powers on earth (Revelation 17:3, 12).

> *seven crowns* (12:3). A sign of authority and false divinity; *diademata* in Greek, as opposed to the word *stephanos,* used for the victory crowns of the woman (Revelation 12:1).

> *tail swept a third of the stars* (12:4). Satan took other angels with him in rebellion against God (Revelation 12:9).

son (12:5). Jesus, the Son of Mary and the Son of God (Isaiah 9:6; Luke 1:35).

snatched up to God (12:5). Ascended to heaven; in contrast to Satan, who is cast out of heaven.

desert (12:6). A place of safety, exile, and testing (John 11:54; Revelation 12:14).

Michael (12:7). An archangel (Jude 9) described as the defender of God's people (Daniel 10:13, 21; 12:1).

accuser (12:10). The literal meaning of the name *Satan,* describing how he works to condemn people and separate them from God (Job 1:9–11; Zechariah 3:1).

wings of a great eagle (12:14). Divine protection (Exodus 19:4; Isaiah 40:31).

serpent spewed water (12:15). Deception and destruction unleashed by Satan like a flood (Psalm 124:2–5; Isaiah 27:1).

earth . . . swallowing the river (12:16). Miraculous rescue by God, who uses creation to defeat Satanic attacks (Numbers 16:26–32).

sea (13:1). Chaos, destruction, and evil separating people from God (Genesis 7:23–24; Exodus 14:26–27; Jude 13).

beast coming out of the sea (13:1). Political oppression, represented as a wild, dangerous, and hostile figure (Job 40:15–41:34; Daniel 7).

ten crowns on his horns (13:1). Royalty and false divinity supported by complete power.

blasphemous name (13:1). An insult to the true God, such as the names of false gods or the title "Lord and God," which the Roman Emperor Domitian assumed (Revelation 17:3).

leopard . . . bear . . . lion (13:2). Three predators that come out of the sea, in reverse order in Daniel 7:4–6, to represent the Greek, Persian, and Babylonian Empires.

fatal wound . . . healed (13:3). The staying power of evil authorities, who return even when thought to be dying, as did the Roman Emperor Caligula (A.D. 37–41).

beast coming out of the earth (13:11). Religious oppression, or the antichrist, also described as a false prophet (Revelation 16:13; 19:20; 20:10).

two horns like a lamb (13:11). The appearance of Christ, the Lamb, with the power of the two witnesses.

spoke like a dragon (13:11). Deceived people on behalf of Satan. The beast uses false religion to secure worship of the political power that authorizes it, as pagan priests did under Rome and others have done since.

miraculous signs (13:13). False miracles used to deceive people, such as those used by Pharaoh's magicians (Exodus 7:22).

right hand or . . . forehead (13:16). Some, marked on the hand, are unaware of doing Satan's work, while others are marked on the forehead, the place of knowledge, since they are aware of whom they serve.

mark of the beast (13:17). Identification as a person devoted to a false god, in contrast to the seal of Christ. Though religious tattoos were common in John's day, the mark is not necessarily physical.

number of the beast (13:18). Either the number equivalent to the name of a person acting as an anti-Christian religious beast or the unholy trinity of Satan, oppression, and deception trying to take the place of God.

Mount Zion (14:1). Heaven, the eternal dwelling of God with His people, represented by the mountain on which the fortress of Jerusalem was built (Galatians 4:26; Hebrews 12:22–24).

defile themselves with women (14:4). To worship false gods, which were often associated with prostitution in the ancient world (Isaiah 57:3–9; Jeremiah 5:7; Hosea 4:10–13).

firstfruits (14:4). A gift of the first and best of a harvest, given to God as an act of worship, recognizing that the whole crop belongs to Him (Exodus 34:26; 2 Chronicles 31:5; Romans 8:23; 1 Corinthians 15:20).

eternal gospel (14:6). The Good News of salvation in Christ, which brings eternal life to all who believe.

Babylon the Great (14:8). The enemy of God's people, represented by the capital of Mesopotamia where the Israelites were exiled, a place notorious for luxury and moral corruption (Psalm 137:8; Isaiah 13:19).

wine of her adulteries (14:8). Spiritual unfaithfulness to God, represented by wine because it is intoxicating at first but leads to tragic foolishness and remorse (Jeremiah 51:6–7; 1 Thessalonians 5:6–9).

wine of God's fury (14:10). Overwhelming judgment on evil, represented by wine because it makes people stagger as though drunk (Isaiah 51:17; Jeremiah 25:15; Psalm 75:7–8).

full strength (14:10). Not tempered by mercy, as wine was often mixed with water. In the past God held back the complete destruction evildoers deserve, but no more.

burning sulfur (14:10). Fire and brimstone, conferring final judgment on God's enemies (Genesis 19:24; Ezekiel 38:22–23) and the ongoing torment of hell (Revelation 19:20; 20:10; 21:8).

seated on the cloud (14:14). Possessing the authority and glory of God (Revelation 14:16).

like a son of man (14:14). Representing Christ, who called Himself the Son of Man (Mark 8:31), and who will fulfill the vision of Daniel 7:13 by "coming with the clouds of heaven" and harvesting believers (Matthew 24:30).

sharp sickle (14:14). Power to cut off lives and gather believers, as stalks of ripe grain were cut and gathered by a curved blade at harvest time (Joel 3:12–16; Mark 4:26–29).

harvest of the earth (14:15). The gathering of all people for judgment, believers and unbelievers together, at the end of the world (Matthew 13:24–30, 36–43).

had charge of the fire (14:18). Authority to work God's judgment (Revelation 8:3–5).

clusters of grapes (14:18). Unbelievers, whose lives gave fruit to the wine of spiritual unfaithfulness (Revelation 14:8) and the wine of God's wrath (Revelation 14:10).

trampled in the winepress (14:20). Crushed by God's judgment, as grapes were stepped on to squeeze out their juice in a large basin (Isaiah 5:1–4; 63:2–6; Joel 3:13).

outside the city (14:20). Outside the place of God's people, the church, who are represented by the city of Jerusalem. Bloodshed inside would defile the city (Hebrews 13:12).

blood flowed . . . high as the horses' bridles (14:20). All unbelievers died and were judged in a scene of unimaginable horror, similar to that in the apocryphal book 1 Enoch 100:1–3.

1,600 stadia (14:20). A symbolic measurement of the entire earth, determined by taking the number of completion squared (10 x 10) times the number of earth squared (4 x 4); this is equal to the approximate length of Palestine.

prostitute (17:1). The religious enemy of God's people, a symbol of unfaithfulness (Deuteronomy 31:16; 2 Chronicles 21:11), in contrast to the faithful woman who gave birth to God's Son (Revelation 12:5) and the church, who will be presented to Christ as a bride (Revelation 19:7–8; 21:2–3).

many waters (17:1). All the peoples, nations, and languages of the earth (Revelation 17:15).

scarlet beast (17:3). The political beast out of the sea (Revelation 13:1–8), in a color usually reserved for the wealthy, though perhaps representing the blood of God's persecuted people (Revelation 12:3).

purple (17:4). The color of wealth or royalty, since purple was an expensive dye (Revelation 18:16).

mystery (17:5). Something that cannot be known unless revealed (Revelation 1:10; 10:7). Many will not recognize the true identity of Babylon, but God's angel reveals it (Revelation 17:8–18).

once was, now is not, and will come (17:8). The political beast that persecutes Christians will reappear after being thought to be dead (Revelation 17:11).

seven hills (17:9). The setting of ancient Rome, representing governments that persecute Christians.

seven kings (17:10). May represent all evil rulers, since they don't match any list of emperors known.

ten kings (17:12). Rulers with complete military might who wage war against God's people for the beast.

one hour (17:12). A very short time; the length of both the reign and ruin of Babylon (Revelation 18:10, 17, 19).

bring her to ruin (17:16). Governments and armies that supported the false religious establishment will despise and turn against it, bringing destruction and humiliation as agents of God's judgment.

home for demons (18:2). An empty and desolate waste, like hell itself.

throw dust on their heads (18:19). A sign of great grief (Job 2:12).

How Is the Devil Defeated? *(10 minutes)*

After the fourth vision presents God's judgment as seven plagues poured out upon the earth, an angel takes John to the desert, the place where the woman of the church has been attacked and is protected from the dragon and his beasts. The religious beast no longer appears to be a lamb but is revealed to be a wealthy prostitute sitting on the political beast, seducing nations into the adultery of unfaithfulness to God, officially supported by the corrupt government. The prostitute's mysterious identity is revealed to be Babylon, the capital of Mesopotamia where the Israelites had been exiled, a place notorious for luxury and moral corruption, and the ancient enemy of God's people (Psalm 137:8; Isaiah 13:19). Although she is called Babylon and the beast she rides is described in terms resembling Rome, together they represent all religious institutions and governments that attack and martyr God's people, since the waters she sits over represent all the peoples, multitudes, nations, and languages (17:18) and she is responsible for the blood of the prophets, the saints, and of all who have been killed on the earth. (18:24).

The prostitute and the beast seem all-powerful and succeed in murdering many of God's people, but they are doomed to destruction. "They will make war against the Lamb, but the Lamb will overcome them because He is Lord of lords and King of kings—and with Him will be His called, chosen and faithful followers" (17:14). The political powers eventually turn against their false religion and act as God's agent of judgment, destroying, humiliating, and consuming the prostitute even as they themselves will be judged and destroyed. The kings and the merchants who grew rich and powerful through the prostitute's deception are only able to weep at her destruction and stand terrified as they face their own impending judgment.

The images are mind-blowing, but the message is clear: The devil has already been defeated by Christ's death and resurrection. Since he can no longer directly attack the church, he continues to work through corrupt governments and false religions to oppress God's people and seduce the nations away from worshipping the true God. The situation of the saints may seem desperate, but we can be sure that Christ, the Lord of lords, will soon avenge our sufferings on earth, bringing judgment and complete destruction on all those who attack the church, blaspheme God, and are intoxicated by wealth and corruption. God will remember all who belong to Him and will give us cause for great rejoicing when He returns in judgment!

Try This: *Spoil Sports*

Share with students a news article that describes a dramatic team sporting event, such as a football, basketball, or baseball game. Ask students to decide which sentences would be difficult to understand if you didn't know the jargon or rules of the game. Are any of the players referred to by a number or a nickname? Is there a description of the response of fans to the victory of their team? What do the team mascots symbolize? Ask students to write a summary of the victory of Christ and His people over Satan and his beasts as if it were a sporting event, the "Saints" versus the "Devils." Tell students to be sure to include Christ's game-winning "touchdown" to earth or "home run" back to heaven, the "fouls," cheating, and bad sportsmanship of Satan, and the response of Christ's 144,000 fans to His victory in contrast to the weeping of Satan's supporters. Allow time for students to share their creative descriptions.

Closing *(2 minutes)*

King of kings, just as You were faithful in sending Your Son, Jesus, to take away Satan's power over us, continue to send Your Spirit to make us faithful in trusting You to the end of time. We pray this through Jesus Christ, our champion. Amen.

woman clothed with the sun **(12:1) Isaiah 54:1; 62:5; Jeremiah 2:2; Luke 1:78–79; Ephesians 5:25; 2 Corinthians 11:2**

moon under her feet **(12:1) Genesis 37:9; 1 Corinthians 15:41; Isaiah 30:26; 1 Kings 5:3; Psalm 8:6; 47:3; Matthew 22:44; Ephesians 1:22; Hebrews 2:7–8**

crown of twelve stars **(12:1) 2 Timothy 2:5; Revelation 1:20**

red dragon **(12:3) Revelation 12:9**

seven heads **(12:3) Revelation 13:1; 17:3**

ten horns **(12:3) Revelation 17:3, 12**

seven crowns **(12:3) Revelation 12:1**

tail swept a third of the stars **(12:4) Revelation 12:9**

son **(12:5) Isaiah 9:6; Luke 1:35**

snatched up to God **(12:5)**

desert **(12:6) John 11:54; Revelation 12:14**

Michael **(12:7) Daniel 10:13, 21; 12:1; Jude 9**

accuser **(12:10) Job 1:9–11; Zechariah 3:1**

wings of a great eagle **(12:14) Exodus 19:4; Isaiah 40:31**

serpent spewed water **(12:15) Psalm 124:2–5; Isaiah 27:1**

earth . . . swallowing the river **(12:16) Numbers 16:26–32**

sea **(13:1) Genesis 7:23–24; Exodus 14:26–27; Jude 13**

beast coming out of the sea **(13:1) Job 40:15–41:34; Daniel 7**

ten crowns on his horns **(13:1)**

blasphemous name **(13:1) Revelation 17:3**

leopard . . . bear . . . lion **(13:2) Daniel 7:4–6**

fatal wound . . . healed **(13:3)**

beast coming out of the earth **(13:11) Revelation 16:13; 19:20; 20:10**

two horns like a lamb **(13:11)**

spoke like a dragon **(13:11)**

miraculous signs **(13:13) Exodus 7:22**

right hand or . . . forehead **(13:16)**

mark . . . of the beast **(13:17)**

number of the beast **(13:18)**

Mount Zion **(14:1) Galatians 4:26; Hebrews 12:22–24**

defile themselves with women **(14:4) Isaiah 57:3–9; Jeremiah 5:7; Hosea 4:10–13**

firstfruits **(14:4) Exodus 34:26; 2 Chronicles 31:5; Romans 8:23; 1 Corinthians 15:20**

eternal gospel **(14:6)**

Babylon the Great **(14:8) Psalm 137:8; Isaiah 13:19**

wine of her adulteries **(14:8) Jeremiah 51:6–7; 1 Thessalonians 5:6–9**

wine of God's fury **(14:10) Isaiah 51:17; Jeremiah 25:15 Psalm 75:7–8**

full strength **(14:10)**

burning sulfur **(14:10) Genesis 19:24; Ezekiel 38:22–23; Revelation 19:20; 20:10; 21:8**

seated on the cloud **(14:14)**

like a son of man **(14:14) Mark 8:31; Daniel 7:13; Matthew 24:30**

sharp sickle **(14:14) Joel 3:12–16; Mark 4:26–29**

harvest of the earth **(14:15) Matthew 13:24–30, 36–43**

had charge of the fire **(14:18) Revelation 8:3–5**

clusters of grapes **(14:18) Revelation 14:8, 10**

trampled in the winepress **(14:20) Isaiah 5:1–4; 63:2–6; Joel 3:13**

outside the city **(14:20) Hebrews 13:12**

blood flowed . . . high as the horses' bridles **(14:20)**

1,600 stadia **(14:20)**

prostitute **(17:1) Deuteronomy 31:16; 2 Chronicles 21:11; Revelation 12:5; 19:7–8; 21:2–3**

many waters **(17:1) Revelation 17:15**

scarlet beast **(17:3) Revelation 13:1–8; 12:3**

purple **(17:4) Revelation 18:16**

mystery **(17:5) Revelation 1:10; 10:7; 17:8–18**

once was, now is not, and will come **(17:8) Revelation 17:11**

seven hills **(17:9)**

seven kings **(17:10)**

ten kings **(17:12)**

one hour **(17:12) Revelation 18:10, 17, 19**

bring her to ruin **(17:16)**

home for demons **(18:2)**

throw dust on their heads **(18:19) Job 2:12**

6

Verifying Victory—
How Will the World End?

REVELATION 19–20

Purpose

Through their study of Revelation, students will begin to understand and anticipate that everyone will be judged and believers will be part of the resurrection at the end of time.

Lesson Outline 6

Activity	Suggested Time	Materials Needed
Opening	2 minutes	None
How Will Christ Return? **Try This:** *Parade Planning*	10 minutes	None None
What Is the Millennium? **Try This:** *Millennium Matching*	20 minutes	Copies of Student Page 6 Bibles
What Are the Two Resurrections? **Try This:** *Resurrection Remembrance*	10 minutes	None Birthday/Baptism cards
What Happens at the Last Judgment? **Try This:** *Righteous Revenge*	10 minutes	None Paper, pens/pencils
What Do the Words Mean? Clues to Chapters 19–20	optional activity	Copies of Vocabulary Page 6, Bibles
Closing	2 minutes	None

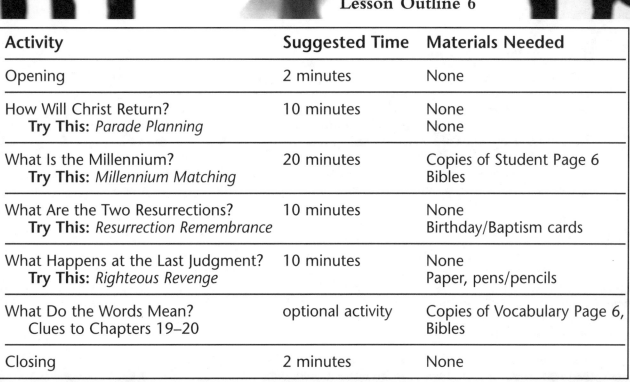

Opening *(2 minutes)*

Faithful and true Lord, strengthen our faith and increase in us the true knowledge of You through this study, so that we remain faithful to the end and true to Your Word, made known to us through Jesus Christ. Amen.

How Will Christ Return? *(10 minutes)*

All the servants of God, in heaven and on earth, will rejoice when Christ returns to judge all people. The world weeps over the end of earthly pleasures in Babylon (18:9–10). But the saints joyfully proclaim Christ's return as the ultimate wedding feast. The faithful celebrate the union of the Son of God as the Bridegroom and the people of God as His bride (19:7). The text contrasts the fine linen of the prostitute (18:16), which is ruined when the political beast strips her naked (17:16), with the bright and clean fine linen of the bride of Christ, which represents the righteous acts of the saints (19:8).

Overwhelmed by the thunderous rejoicing and tremendous reward that awaits believers, John falls down to worship at the feet of the angel who is speaking God's Word to him. The angel forcefully warns John to stop and worship God only. John's lapse is a lesson for us: no matter how thankful we are for God's message, we are never to worship the messenger! The only messenger worthy of our praise is Christ Himself.

John then sees heaven open and Christ Himself appear. Although Jesus came first as a humble servant and friend of sinners, He will return as a mighty warrior, the victorious leader of the righteous armies of heaven, judging and destroying His enemies. Although Christ entered Jerusalem peacefully on Palm Sunday, riding a donkey, He will return to conquer on a white battle horse. In contrast to the prostitute of false religion, Jesus is called "Faithful and True," the Word of God. Christ has a name known only to Himself, the King of kings and Lord of lords. In contrast to the white rider of human conquest (6:2), Jesus wears many crowns and a robe dipped in the blood of His own sacrifice. He strikes down the nations with the word of His mouth and offers the corpses of all His enemies as supper for all the birds of the sky. In the end, the most powerful human governments, religious deceivers, and all the kings of the earth together will not be able to stand or escape from the Word of God, revealed in Christ Jesus.

Try This: *Parade Planning*

Ask students, "Have you ever been in a parade? If you could ride on a float in any parade with any celebrities, heroes, or dignitaries, what parade would you choose, and with whom?" (Answers will vary.) **"How will Christ's return be like the parade honoring a conqueror?"** (It will be a celebration of victory for believers.) **"How will it be like a wedding reception?"** (We will enter into the very presence of the Christ, the Bridegroom, with the same bliss a newly married couple experiences.) **"How are the two alike?"** (The wedding feast of the Bridegroom will be an ongoing celebration of the victory won for us in Christ.)

What Is the Millennium? *(20 minutes)*

Revelation 20 is a source of great controversy, much of it resulting from confusion and disagreement over the meaning of the "thousand years" *(millennium)*. The millennium is the period of a thousand years, mentioned in verses 2–7, during which Satan will be bound and true believers will reign with God as priests. Following the millennium, the dead will be raised and Satan will be released to be destroyed in a final battle against God. Attempts to understand the millennium have generally resulted in three kinds of interpretations.

Distribute copies of Student Page 6 to each student. Have students fill in their outlines as you review the three most common interpretations of the millennium.

Premillennialism is the view that Christ will return to earth before *(pre-)* a literal thousand-year period of Christian rule on earth *(millennium)*. This view sees Revelation as a straight time line: not a cycle of visions describing the same events, but a series of similar events occurring one after another. In this view, Christ will return twice, and there will be two physical resurrections. Christ's first return will mark "the rapture," when the bodies of dead believers will be resurrected and living believers will suddenly disappear from earth to celebrate the wedding feast of the Lamb in heaven. While the saints are enjoying the feast, those left behind on earth suffer under the rule of the antichrist during a period known as "the great tribulation." Christ will bring the saints when He returns a second time to defeat the antichrist, bind Satan, and begin a literal thousand-year reign on earth. After the millennium, Satan will be released to deceive the nations again and gather new enemies of God. Christ will defeat these new enemies and cast Satan into the lake of fire. Then the unbelieving dead will be raised in a second resurrection, the final judgment will occur, and God will create a new heaven and earth.

Premillennial View

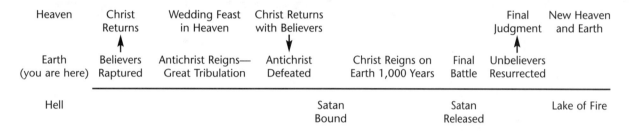

Postmillennialism is the view that Christ will return to earth after *(post-)* a symbolic period of Christian rule on earth *(millennium)*. This view sees the millennium not as a literal thousand years but as representing the entire period from the first coming of Christ to His return. During that time the reign of believers with Christ will gradually emerge as the church grows and influences most people in the world to become Christians. As a result, Satan will be bound, in the sense that evil will be subdued and good will triumph. Then Christ will return to resurrect the dead, judge all people, and create a new heaven and earth.

Postmillennial View

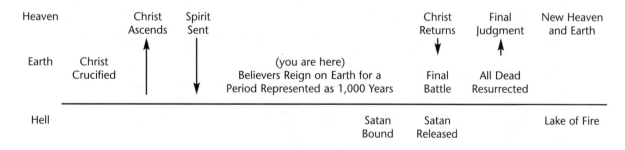

Amillennialism is the view that there is no (the prefix *a* in Greek is like *not* in English) period of Christian rule on earth *(millennium)*. This view sees the thousand years as symbolically representing the entire period from the first coming of Christ to His return. This interpretation understands the reign and priestly service of believers with Christ as a description of the situation in heaven, not on earth, during this period. Or, more often it represents the spiritual rule of Christ through His means of grace, the Word and the Sacraments, which govern the hearts and minds of believers with the Spirit's love, hope, peace, and joy in spite of outward circumstances. Satan has already been bound by the victory of Christ, though he will be released to deceive and gather the numerous unbelievers for battle and judgment at the end of the world.

Amillennial View

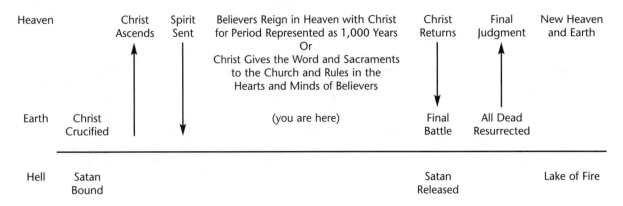

Although many of the end-times books, movies, and speakers popular today take a premillennial view, the most widely held interpretation throughout history has been amillennialism. Along with postmillennialism, it most faithfully follows the nonlinear nature of apocalyptic literature, recognizing the tendency of apocalyptic literature to loop back and repeat the telling of events from a different perspective. John does not introduce his vision of the thousand years with the time reference "after this," as he often does in other chapters to indicate a sequence of events. So there is no reason to believe that the binding of Satan is different than his defeat and being cast out of heaven (12:7–9) or that Christ's return, described as unique in the rest of Scripture, will actually occur twice (1 Corinthians 15:51–52). Nor does John ever say that the reign of the saints will occur on earth. Since John refers to them as "the souls of those who had been beheaded" (20:4), it would seem that the reign would be in heaven, where the saints are awaiting the judgment (6:9–11).

Try This: *Millennium Matching*

Have students look up these Scriptures, which deal with *eschatology*, the end times: Matthew 24:3–35; 1 Corinthians 15:22–27, 51–57; 2 Peter 3:8–10. What information does each passage give about how the world will end? (The images in Matthew are very similar to those used in Revelation. The Corinthians passages focus on the resurrection of the dead. 2 Peter is clear that God does not mark time in the way that we do.) **How does each passage support or refute views of what the millennium might be like?** (All of the passages speak of the second coming of Christ as being a future event. The resurrection of the dead is a one-time event, and our understanding of how God marks time is limited by our human knowledge.)

What Are the Two Resurrections? *(10 minutes)*

If Christ will only return once to raise the living and the dead, as the rest of the Bible seems to indicate (John 5:28–29; 1 Corinthians 15:12–28; 1 Thessalonians 4:14–16), what does John mean when he talks about "the first resurrection" and says that "the rest of the dead did not come to life until the thousand years were ended" (20:5–6)? Although no other Scriptures use the term "first resurrection," some do speak of two types of resurrection. The first, coming to faith in Christ (most often at Baptism), is a spiritual resurrection that occurs before the second, the physical resurrection of our bodies on the Last Day (John 5:25; 11:23–26; Ephesians 2:1–6; Colossians 3:1–4; Romans 6:1–5; 1 Peter 4:6).

This interpretation helps explain what John means when he says the "second death" has no power over those who have part in the first resurrection. Since the second death is defined as eternal punishment and destruction in the lake of fire (20:14), it follows that those whose souls have been made alive with Christ in this life need not worry about eternal punishment. They may experience the death of their bodies, but as a result of the first resurrection, which is a gift of faith in Christ, believers won't experience the death of their souls at the second resurrection, when all the dead will be raised to face God's judgment. "The rest of the dead," those whose spirits have not been made alive with Christ, do not reign with Christ as they await the end of the world, but will be raised on Judgment Day to stand before God and meet their eternal condemnation.

Try This: *Resurrection Remembrance*

Bring in samples of birthday and/or Baptism cards. Ask students about some ways people try to make birthdays memorable. (Answers will vary, but could include parties, gifts, cards, etc.) What are some ways you could mark and remember your first resurrection day? (Answers will vary. Some students may celebrate Baptism birthdays at home; ask them to share how their families celebrate.) Encourage students to find ways to celebrate and remember the date of their Baptism. They may want to plan a party, make a cake, or create some other remembrance for that day. If students don't know the date of their Baptism, encourage them to research and find out when it was. Be aware of students who may not have been baptized. This discussion may provide an opportunity to share more about faith in Christ with these individuals and—as appropriate—encourage them to be baptized.

What Happens at the Last Judgment? *(10 minutes)*

When the time comes for the end of the world, Satan will no longer attack the church through the political beast and the false prophet, which will have been cast into the lake of fire. Instead, he will be released from his prison to personally gather the armies of those who oppose Christ from all over the earth. Though Satan has deceived people as numerous "as the sand on the seashore," who think that they can and must destroy God's people, the final battle is entirely one-sided: "fire came down from heaven and devoured them" (20:9). The devil is thrown into the lake of fire, a place of permanent torment from which there is no escape. Earth and sky flee from God's throne, most likely indicating the destruction of the present heaven and earth. The creation of a new heaven and earth will leave no room for them. Death and Hades (the Greek term for the place of the dead) are destroyed by being thrown into the lake of fire, the final destination for anything that is not part of God's eternal kingdom.

This destruction leaves no place for the bodies and souls of people to stand except before the throne of God, where they are judged. Books, which hold a record of all the things anyone has done, are opened. According to these books, all are condemned. God is a holy God, only the holy can live with Him, and no amount of good works can cover over even a single sin we have committed. Thankfully, the eternal destiny of the faithful is based on another book that is opened—the Book of Life. This book records the identities of those forgiven and granted eternal life through faith in Christ and the salvation He earned through His work on the cross. Those who are not recorded in the Book of Life are cast into the lake of fire. But those who put their trust in God will spend eternity with Him in the new heaven and earth.

Try This: *Righteous Revenge*

Have students make a list of all the movies they can think of that feature a person or group of people who have been mistreated coming back to take revenge on their attackers. Are any of the methods of revenge violent? Were these people justified by the seriousness of the wrong being avenged? Why will God, who wants all people to be saved (1 Timothy 2:4), eventually return to destroy those who have rejected Him and attacked His people? (While God desires all to be saved, He is a God of justice, and He will demand that all receive what is due to them. Thankfully, since He has made us His baptized children, He sees only the merits of Christ in us.)

What Do the Words Mean? Clues to Chapters 19–20 (optional activity)

Distribute copies of Vocabulary Page 6 to students. Encourage students to work together to study each of the terms listed. Students may use the verses given to find other examples of the terms used in Scripture.

wedding of the Lamb (19:7). The joyous celebration when the church joins Christ forever in heaven; often portrayed as a wedding feast (Matthew 22:2; 25:1–13; Luke 12:35–36; Revelation 19:9).

bride (19:7). God's people, the church (Isaiah 62:5; Jeremiah 2:2; John 3:29; Revelation 21:2, 9; 22:17).

robe dipped in blood (19:13). Not the blood of enemies about to be slain, but Christ's own blood, in which the saints have washed their robes (Revelation 7:15); displayed as a sin offering for others (Leviticus 8:14–15).

standing in the sun (19:17). Reflecting the glory of Christ (Revelation 1:16; 10:1).

great supper of God (19:17). The gathering of birds to eat the corpses of God's enemies, in contrast to the wedding feast of the Lamb; a shocking but fitting judgment on those who persecuted believers (Psalm 79:1–2).

false prophet (19:20). Another name for the harlot or religious beast (Revelation 16:13; 20:10).

lake of burning sulfur (19:20). Hell, the place of permanent destruction (Revelation 20:10; 21:8) also known as the lake of fire (Revelation 20:14–15).

key to the Abyss (20:1). Authority to lock Satan in hell, though Satan will be released shortly before the final judgment (Revelation 9:1).

bound him for a thousand years (20:2). God limited Satan's power for a complete period of time, the time from Jesus' resurrection until Satan is released to be destroyed at the final judgment (Jude 6).

reigned with Christ a thousand years (20:4). Sat enthroned and exercised authority as saints in Christ's presence from the time of their death to the physical resurrection and final judgment (2 Timothy 2:11–12).

first resurrection (20:5–6). The spiritual resurrection of believers through faith (Romans 6:1–8; Ephesians 2:4–6; 1 Peter 2:24), by which their spirits reign in heaven even before the physical resurrection.

priests of God (20:6). Servants allowed to enter God's presence (1 Peter 2:5, 9; Revelation 1:6; 5:10).

Gog and Magog (20:8). All the unbelieving people, represented by Gog, prince of Meshech and Tubal, and Magog, his tribe, who arouse God's anger by attacking His people and are destroyed (Ezekiel 38–39).

Closing *(2 minutes)*

Holy God, You wait to destroy all Your enemies, including sin and death, so that more people may come to know Your salvation. Send us to spread the message of resurrection to our family and friends, so that they, too, may be immune from eternal death. We ask this through Christ Jesus. Amen.

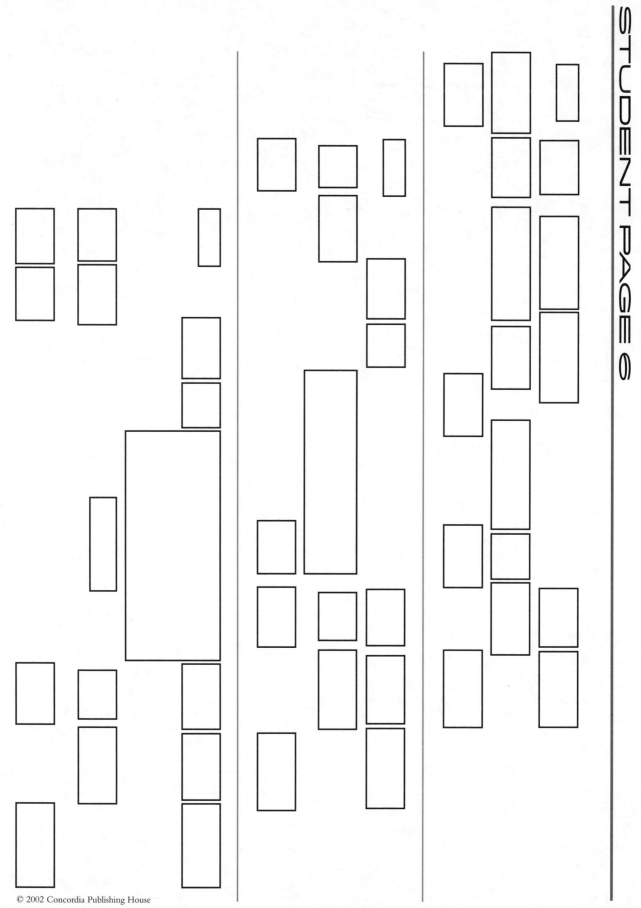

wedding of the Lamb **(19:7) Matthew 22:2; 25:1–13; Luke 12:35–36; Revelation 19:9**

bride **(19:7) Isaiah 62:5; Jeremiah 2:2; John 3:29; Revelation 21:2, 9; 22:17**

robe dipped in blood **(19:13) Revelation 7:15; Leviticus 8:14–15**

standing in the sun **(19:17) Revelation 1:16; 10:1**

great supper of God **(19:17) Psalm 79:1–2**

false prophet **(19:20) Revelation 16:13; 20:10**

lake of burning sulfur **(19:20) Revelation 20:10; 21:8; 20:14–15**

key to the Abyss **(20:1) Revelation 9:1**

bound him for a thousand years **(20:3) Jude 6**

reigned with Christ a thousand years **(20:4) 2 Timothy 2:11–12**

first resurrection **(20:5–6) Romans 6:1–8; Ephesians 2:4–6; 1 Peter 2:24**

priests of God **(20:6) 1 Peter 2:5, 9; Revelation 1:6; 5:10**

Gog and Magog **(20:8) Ezekiel 38–39**

Picturing Paradise—
What Will Eternity Be Like?

Purpose

Believers have no reason to fear the future. God's own children can look forward to an eternity vastly different from and superior to this earthly life.

Lesson Outline 7

Activity	Suggested Time	Materials Needed
Opening	2 minutes	None
What Will Paradise Be Like? **Try This:** *Picture Perfect*	15 minutes	None Vacation photos
What Will Be Missing in Eternity? **Try This:** *Heavenly Hoaxes*	20 minutes	None Copies of Student Page 7
What Will You Do There? **Try This:** *Dream Developments*	15 minutes	None Newsprint, markers
Closing	2 minutes	None

Opening *(2 minutes)*

Eternal God, You are the Alpha and the Omega, the beginning and the end of all things. Enable us to focus on You as we study Your Word so that we can understand and thank You for the wonderful gifts You have given us. This we ask in Jesus Christ. Amen.

What Will Paradise Be Like? *(15 minutes)*

After witnessing the judgment of all people and the destruction of evil, John is shown a preview of the paradise where believers will spend eternity. Since all creation has suffered devastation and decay as a result of human sin and the perversions of evil (Romans 8:19–23), God will create a new heaven and a new earth, restored to His original design, when sin and evil are destroyed forever (2 Peter 3:13). The centerpiece of the new creation will be a new Jerusalem, as promised in Isaiah 65:17–19. The new holy city will not resemble the historic human city and will certainly not be built by human effort. Instead, it will come "down out of heaven from God" (21:2) and will represent the holy presence of God with His perfected people.

The beauty and glory of the new arrangement is represented by the design of the new Jerusalem. The city shines like fantastically pure gold and every kind of precious jewel, reflecting the brilliance and perfection of God's glory. Unlike the earthly Jerusalem, God's creation is perfectly symmetrical, as tall as it is wide as it is high. Its vast dimensions, 12,000 stadia (about 1,375 miles or 2,220 kilometers) cubed, represent the completeness (10x10x10) of the church (x12) it contains. The 12 gates, named for the 12 tribes of Israel, and the 12 foundations, named for the 12 apostles, represent the unity and completeness of God's Word and God's people of the Old and New Testaments who are saved by it. The thickness of the walls, 144 cubits (about 200 feet or 65 meters), represents the church (12x12) and the perfect safety in which God's people will live. The safety comes not from the walls themselves, since the gate is always open, but from the continuous presence of God and His light.

There will be no more death, mourning, crying, or pain, because those who dwell in the city will be eternally cured of sin and its side effects, both spiritual and physical. God's people will be fully human but also perfectly obedient, as Christ was on earth. Among the things God will make new are the physical bodies of believers, which will be resurrected and recreated regardless of where or how they were laid to rest (20:13). Our new bodies will be recognizable and fully physical but also miraculous and immortal, as Christ's body was after His resurrection (Luke 24:36–43; 1 Corinthians 15:35–54).

Try This: *Picture Perfect*

Pull out and share some of your favorite vacation photos with your students. Ask, "Have you ever enjoyed a vacation so much you considered it to be like heaven on earth? Where were you? Whom were you with? What made it so great?" Have students close their eyes and try to imagine that vacation made even better: with no hassles, conflicts, sins, or evil, with perfect weather and unimaginable beauty, with God visibly present to protect and provide for them, with perfect physical and spiritual health, and with no return to any kind of daily grind. Ask students to share their vision of paradise with someone else by drawing or describing it. How does it compare to the vision John describes? (Answers will vary.)

What Will Be Missing in Eternity? *(20 minutes)*

John sees heaven both in terms of the wonders of God's presence and the absence of anything evil or opposed to God. As John describes the passing away of the first heaven and earth, he mentions that there is no longer any sea. It is unclear if this is to be understood literally; it may be another attempt at describing the unknown. John has already described a sea of glass around God's throne (4:6) and will soon describe the river of the waters of life, which would be expected to flow to a larger body of water. John may be using the sea as an image of chaos, destruction, and evil, those things that threaten our survival and separate people from God (Genesis 7:23–24; Exodus 14:26–28; Psalm 89:9; Jude 13).

Also absent from heaven are "the cowardly, the unbelieving, the vile, the murderers, the sexually immoral, those who practice magic arts, the idolaters and all liars—their place will be in the fiery lake of burning sulfur" (Revelation 21:8). Christ's warning would be a message of despair if it were intended to be a shopping list of unforgivable acts, since few of us could honestly examine our thoughts and lives without recognizing at least some of these sins. However, the point is not that anyone who ever committed any of these will be excluded from the new Jerusalem; rather, the point is that these things separate us from God and so must be overcome by the cleansing blood of Christ and the sustaining waters of Holy Baptism. Those who believe in Christ receive power to become the children of God and to inherit a place in His kingdom, but those who willingly persist in such sins have rejected their inheritance. The dwelling of God with us demands the absence of sin: "Nothing impure will ever enter it, nor will anyone who does what is shameful or deceitful, but only those whose names are written in the Lamb's book of life" (Revelation 21:27).

In addition to evil and sin, the temple and the sun are also missing. In heaven both are no longer necessary. The temple was where Israelites went to make sacrifices for their sins and enter the presence of God. Christ's sacrifice was a once-and-for-all solution to sin, however, and no further sacrifices are needed. Nor will believers need a place to enter God's presence, because they will never leave it. Instead of the sun, which comes and goes and is a created thing, residents of heaven will bask continually in the sustaining light of the Lamb, the light of the world.

Try This: *Heavenly Hoaxes*

Distribute copies of Student Page 7. Popular movies, books, songs, and jokes often present heaven in ways that are contrary to what Scripture reveals. Have students work through the statements alone or in small groups. When they have completed their work, review their findings together.

1. **All dogs go to heaven—Revelation 22:15** (False; they are outside the walls of the city.)

2. **The New Jerusalem has pearly gates—Revelation 21:21** (True; each of the 12 gates is made of pearl.)

3. **St. Peter stands at the gate—Revelation 21:12** (False; gates are guarded by angels.)

4. **You take a quiz to get in—Revelation 21:27** (False; your name is recorded in the Book of Life.)

5. **You become an angel—Matthew 22:30** (False; we may be *like* angels, but we do not become angels. See 1 Corinthians 15:42–44.)

6. **You get a harp to play—Revelation 15:2** (True; for some of those in the next life.)

7. **You get wings for transportation—Revelation 21:24** (False; we get to walk.)

8. **Everything in heaven is white—Revelation 4:3** (False; heaven is described as every color of the rainbow.)

9. **The streets are made of gold—Revelation 21:21** (True; at least the streets have the appearance of gold.)

10. **In heaven there is no beer (or wine)—Matthew 26:29** (True and false; while beer is not mentioned, Jesus does refer to drinking the "fruit of the vine" in His Father's kingdom.)

What Will You Do There? *(15 minutes)*

John's final description of the new heaven and earth in the first verses of chapter 22 in some ways resembles the Garden of Eden, where human history and the biblical account began. Just as Eden was watered by a river flowing from its center (Genesis 2:10), so the new paradise is watered by the river of the water of life flowing along its main street, an image Jesus used for the Holy Spirit (John 7:38). Just as immortality in Eden came from the tree of life in its midst (Genesis 2:9), so the new paradise sustains and heals the nations with a continual crop from the tree of life, or possibly from a grove of such trees, watered by the river. The very word *paradise* comes from a Persian word meaning "garden." John's description of paradise returns us to a place where God walks and talks with His people, providing all they need and keeping them in perfect peace.

Yet the new paradise is not only a garden; it is at the same time a city. The creation of a new Jerusalem within the new heaven and earth suggests that God has taken the best features of human civilization and combined them with the original perfection of Eden to create a new paradise, where He lives in the midst of His people. The curse of sin, all of life's difficulties, death, and our devastating separation from God are gone forever. The best parts of our present world, including the joys we experience here, physical life itself, and the togetherness we share as His people, are ours forever.

What will we do as residents of the new garden city? We will serve God, and we will reign with Him forever. We will see God face-to-face and live as His people, as we were intended to live. While we can only imagine exactly what that will involve, John's description assures us that it will be wonderfully thrilling, perfectly joyful, and absolutely fitting for each of us.

Try This: *Dream Developments*

Ask students to try to answer one of the following questions:

1. **If you could combine the best features of living in a great city with the best parts of living in the country, and could locate your development in any kind of outdoor landscape, what would your neighborhood be like?**

2. **If you could combine the best features of an awesome worship service with the best party imaginable, and could invite anyone, what would the experience be like?**

3. **If you could combine all of the things you most enjoy doing with an ideal position serving God in heaven, what would your job description be like?**

Allow student to work in small groups and use newsprint and markers to outline or describe their "paradise." Allow time for sharing with the whole group. What hopes for heaven do these daydreams reflect? Why should we think about these things (Philippians 4:8)? (Answers will vary. In Philippians 4:8 we are told to think on positive attributes.)

Closing *(2 minutes)*

Light of the world, thank You for sending Jesus to overcome the sins that separated us from eternal life with You in heaven. Empower us through Your Spirit to joyfully serve You here on earth until we see You face to face. In Jesus Christ we pray. Amen.

Heavenly Hoaxes

Popular movies, books, songs, and jokes often present heaven in ways that are contrary to what Scripture reveals. Which of the following stereotypes about heaven are true, according to Scripture, and which are false? If you don't know for sure, look up the Bible verse that follows each example. What are some other popular misconceptions about heaven?

1. All dogs go to heaven	true	false	**Revelation 22:15**
2. The New Jerusalem has pearly gates	true	false	**Revelation 21:21**
3. St. Peter stands at the gate	true	false	**Revelation 21:12**
4. You take a quiz to get in	true	false	**Revelation 21:27**
5. You become an angel	true	false	**Matthew 22:30**
6. You get a harp to play	true	false	**Revelation 15:2**
7. You get wings for transportation	true	false	**Revelation 21:24**
8. Everything in heaven is white	true	false	**Revelation 4:3**
9. The streets are made of gold	true	false	**Revelation 21:21**
10. In heaven there is no beer (or wine)	true	false	**Matthew 26:29**

Making It Mine— What Does Revelation Mean for My Life?

REVELATION 22:6–21

Purpose

As young people read the closing words of Christ's revelation to John, they can begin to integrate the warnings and encouragement of Revelation into their life's plans and priorities.

Activity	Suggested Time	Materials Needed
Opening	2 minutes	None
How Can You Be Ready for What's Coming? **Try This:** *Inheritance Implications*	10 minutes	Bibles *Imagine* CD (optional)
How Can You Face the Future without Fear? **Try This:** *Prominent Promises*	20 minutes	Bibles Copies of Student Page 8
What's Your Bottom Line? **Try This:** *Deliberate Differences*	20 minutes	Bibles Newsprint, markers
Closing	2 minutes	None

Opening (2 minutes)

God of the prophets, speak to our hearts through Your revelation, so that we are ready for Your return and able to face the future without fear. Strengthen our spirits through Your Spirit, so that we truly hear and keep Your Word. This we pray through Jesus Christ. Amen.

How Can You Be Ready for What's Coming? *(10 minutes)*

Read Revelation 22:6–10. Having described the end of the world and the promised paradise, Revelation concludes with a series of short, encouraging messages that tie the revelation together, summarize its major themes, and urge its readers to be ready for Christ's return. Just as John began by explaining how he received the revelation by means of an angel sent from God, so he ends by reminding readers that the visions came by means of an angel. The angel was from "the God of the spirits of the prophets," and therefore this revelation can be trusted to be as true as anything in Scripture. Just as the first verses of Revelation bless those who take these words to heart and warn that the time is near, so the last verses warn that Christ is coming soon and bless those who keep the words of its prophecy.

Two important and complementary themes in Revelation are (1) that the visions given John are trustworthy and true and (2) that we are to live in response to these visions. It is one thing to intellectually believe the words of God to be accurate. It is another thing to read, mark, learn, and take them to heart in such a way that they make a difference in what we believe and do. It is not enough to act like a Christian if we don't really trust what God's Word reveals about Christ. John unwittingly illustrates the connection between the two when he once again falls down to worship at the feet of the angel who is showing him the visions. Once again the angel rebukes John and reminds him to worship God alone, recognizing the awesome and unrivaled glory of God! We, too, are reminded to worship only the true God in response to His gifts of enduring love and eternal life.

The angel instructs John not to seal up but to reveal the words of prophecy, because the time is near. What God reveals about Himself and the future is not given us to hide but to share with others, so that they can be ready when the time comes to meet Him face-to-face. This is to be the primary mission of all those who believe God's Word to be true: not to qualify and enforce proper behavior in this world, but to enable people to qualify for the world to come through the salvation brought by Jesus. That seems to be what the angel is getting at when he says, "Let him who does wrong continue to do wrong; let him who is vile continue to be vile; let him who does right continue to do right; and let him who is holy continue to be holy" (22:11). It's not that God doesn't care about evil—quite the opposite: He was crucified to conquer it and will return to remove it! But evil will continue to exist in our world until the bitter end, and we should not expect otherwise. Rather than being overly focused on behavior, we are called to make sure others have the Savior!

Try This: *Inheritance Implications*

As a discussion starter you may want to share the music and/or lyrics of the song "Imagine" by John Lennon from the album *Imagine*. Lennon's influential song urges listeners to "imagine there's no heaven" and suggests that living for the present will cause all the people of the world to live in harmony. John the apostle certainly would have argued the opposite, that God's grace, forgiveness, and the certainty of heaven motivates believers to live unselfishly here on earth, devoting their lives to meeting the needs of others, without despairing about the continued existence of evil. Ask students, "What do you think? In Revelation does the vision of the fantastic inheritance we will receive make us 'so heavenly minded we're no earthly good,' or does it in fact motivate us to 'store up treasure in heaven' by working for peace and grace rather than personal gain here on earth?"

How Can You Face the Future without Fear? *(20 minutes)*

Read Revelation 22:11–16. Following the final message of the angel, John's telling of the revelation gives way to the voice of Christ, who speaks a series of promises that are intended to bring courage to all Christians. First we are reassured that Christ is coming soon and will reward those who have worked and suffered on His behalf. The fact that it has been nearly two thousand years since Christ announced that He would return soon should not surprise us, since Scripture declares, "With the Lord a day is like a thousand years, and a thousand years are like a day" (2 Peter 3:8). Peter assures us that the delay is for our benefit: "The Lord is not slow in keeping His promise, as some understand slowness. He is patient with you, not wanting anyone to perish, but everyone to come to repentance. But the day of the Lord will come like a thief" (2 Peter 3:9–10). Christ Himself did not know the time of His return (Matthew 24:36), but from the perspective of eternity it will certainly be soon. From a human perspective Christ's return may also seem soon, since our life can end at any moment. When the Last Day will occur (from a historical perspective) is irrelevant; what is important is to know that it will be soon, that "our salvation is nearer now than when we first believed" (Romans 13:11). For those in pain, who are afraid that their suffering will be endless, the promise that Christ's return will be soon is a source of strength and courage.

In a similar way, those who are afraid of the end of the world, or even the end of their life, can find comfort in Christ's assurance that He is "the Alpha and the Omega, the First and the Last, the Beginning and the End" (Revelation 22:13). Just as Jesus was involved in our creation and accomplished our salvation, so He assures our resurrection and preservation after the destruction of our bodies and our world.

"Those who wash their robes" (22:14) are those faithful believers who have had sins forgiven because of Christ's blood, shed in their place. Christ's gift entitles believers to immortality and fellowship with God in the new heaven in spite of their sins, so that they need not fear facing the wrath of God's judgment. Although "we were by nature objects of wrath . . . because of His great love for us, God, who is rich in mercy, made us alive with Christ even when we were dead in transgressions. . . . God raised us up with Christ and seated us with Him in the heavenly realms in Christ Jesus, in order that in the coming ages He might show the incomparable riches of His grace, expressed in His kindness to us in Christ Jesus" (Ephesians 2:3–7).

"Those who practice magic arts, the sexually immoral, the murderers, the idolaters and everyone who loves and practices falsehood" (Revelation 22:15) will be excluded from life with God. This warns that all who take sin lightly will not be a part of the new life. Believers, however, need not fear that any persecution, corruption, or addiction will afflict us in the new heaven and earth.

Christ's return will usher in a new and brighter world for us, as the return of the morning star brings the light of a new day. As the root of David's family tree, Jesus created this world; but as the offspring of David, He obtained a new world for us through His death and resurrection. Therefore, no matter what the future holds, we need not fear, because "if God is for us, who can be against us?" (Romans 8:31).

Try This: *Prominent Promises*

Distribute copies of Student Page 8. Allow students to work in small groups to complete the activity. Allow time for groups to share their insights.

The word *blessed* is often used in Scripture to point out the promises of God. The most famous examples are the Beatitudes (from the Latin word for *blessed*) in Matthew 5:3–12, promises made by Jesus to those who suffer for His sake. There are also seven significant "blessed" statements scattered throughout Revelation that point out the promises of God. After looking up each one, write down the answers to three questions: (1) Who is considered blessed? (2) Why? (3) What does it mean for me?

Suggested answers are given below; students' answers to what this means for them will vary.

Revelation 1:3—Those who read the revelation and take it to heart. The end is near.

Revelation 14:13—The dead who died in the Lord. They will rest from their labor.

Revelation 16:15—The watchful/awake. They will not be shamefully exposed.

Revelation 19:9—Those invited to the wedding feast. They will inherit eternal life.

Revelation 20:6—The holy from the first resurrection (baptized). Second death has no power over them.

Revelation 22:7—He who keeps the words of the prophecy. Unspecified blessings.

Revelation 22:14—The faithful who wash their robes in the blood of the Lamb. They will inherit the tree of life.

What's Your Bottom Line? *(20 minutes)*

Read Revelation 22:17–21. The last words of teachers and coaches just before a competition begins are often carefully chosen to encourage the best performance possible. They summarize prior instructions, calm fears, and urge the competitors to focus on the bottom line, the key that will make the difference between winning and losing, by restating the purpose and desired outcome of all that's gone before.

The bottom line for many who read Revelation is to join in the final response of the Holy Spirit and the bride of Christ, His people: "Come!" It is an exclamation of exhilaration, a pleading prayer, and an outburst of obedience all rolled into one, as when players ready for the game shout together, "Let's go!" Those who know the joy of reconciliation with God, which came through Jesus' death and resurrection, are ready and waiting—even anxious—for His return and the remaking of the world. They look forward to a perfect paradise, where all people can live in the presence and provision of God. "Amen. Come, Lord Jesus" (Revelation 22:20).

Yet others still thirst for the joy and assurance of the salvation won by Christ. To them, Christ speaks and says, "Come! Whoever is thirsty, let him come; and whoever wishes, let him take the free gift of the water of life" (22:17). It is the same invitation recorded in John's account of Jesus' life: "If anyone is thirsty, let him come to Me and drink. Whoever believes in Me, as the Scripture has said, streams of living water will flow from within him" (John 7:37–38). The water of life is the Holy Spirit of God, which works faith in us and draws others to faith through us. Out of gratitude to God for quenching our aching thirst, we share His Word of grace and forgiveness, which invites others to "Come!" and discover a quencher for their thirst.

The bottom line for some is a warning not to add to or subtract from what God has revealed. Such corruption will be punished because it leads people away from the eternal life and fellowship with God described in Revelation. Our curious, fallen, sinful nature has caused many people to add speculations and sensational theories about the unclear passages of Revelation. Sometimes its clear messages are hidden. At other times, our weakness makes us want to ignore or eliminate the parts of God's revelation that we find confusing, convicting, or disagreeable. At such times, John warns us to beware, lest we lose the gifts of forgiveness, freedom, and fellowship with God that have been won for us in Christ.

Ultimately, that free gift, the grace of the Lord Jesus, is the bottom line for all of us, in Revelation as throughout Scripture. Until Christ returns, the grace of the Lord Jesus with God's people is the hope of the world, the light that brings light to our hearts and enables us to fearlessly, faithfully face the future.

Try This: *Deliberate Differences*

Ask students to make a list of the messages or symbols that have been especially meaningful to them as they have read through Revelation. Ask, "What have these images meant for you? What difference do they make in how you will face the future and live from now on?" (Since we are God's redeemed children we know our future is secure, and we can face the challenges of everyday living with confidence.) **Encourage students to make a poster of their favorite image to put up where they can see it each day, reminding them of what they've discovered in Revelation, and how, strengthened by the Spirit, they intend to live as a result.**

Closing *(2 minutes)*

Alpha and Omega, Beginning and End, thank You for the washing of forgiveness given through Your death and resurrection, which has begun a new life in us. Fill us with Your grace, so that we are able to share the water of life with all who are thirsty, until the morning star dawns and the world itself is made new. In Your name, Jesus, we pray. Amen.

Prominent Promises

The word *blessed* is often used in Scripture to point out the promises of God. The most famous examples are the Beatitudes (from the Latin word for *blessed*) in Matthew 5:3–12, promises made by Jesus to those who suffer for His sake. There are also seven significant "blessed" statements scattered throughout Revelation that point out the promises of God. After looking up each one, write down the answers to three questions: (1) Who is considered blessed? (2) Why? (3) What does it mean for me?

	Who?	Why?	What about me?
Revelation 1:3			
Revelation 14:13			
Revelation 16:15			
Revelation 19:9			
Revelation 20:6			
Revelation 22:7			
Revelation 22:14			

Glossary of Terms and Images in Revelation

Although John speaks plainly when he refers to himself in Revelation, he uses a great deal of symbolic language and many metaphors to describe the appearance of Christ. This is not surprising when we consider that human words were invented to describe our lives on this earth but are inadequate at describing the things of God. The picture John describes seems strange to us, but most of the symbolism is found in and explained by other prophetic visions in Scripture, producing a powerful image of the eternal power and glory of Christ Jesus.

In order to help explain the various symbolism and imagery used in each section of Revelation, a glossary of numbers and phrases follows. The suggested definitions are based on Scripture and are considered a "most probable" meaning for that term. The suggested Scriptures may be explained in further study.

3. The number of God (the Holy Trinity: Father, Son, and Holy Spirit; the same yesterday, today, and forever) or evil trying to displace God through an unholy trinity.

3½. The number of evil and brokenness (broken perfection, half the perfect number 7); often used to describe an evil time, as in 3½ years, the equivalent of 42 months or 1,260 days.

4. The number of the earth (4 directions, 4 seasons, 4 corners of the earth).

6. The number of evil and incompleteness (1 less than 7), and perhaps the number to represent humanity, created on the 6th day. Great evil is 666 (the number of evil or humankind trying to appear triune, like God).

7. The number of completion and absolute perfection or holiness (7 days of creation, 7 days in a week, the 7th day devoted to worship), or the reunion of God with the earth (3 + 4) through a covenant of grace.

10. The number of completion and perfection (10 fingers, 10 toes) brought about by God (3 + 7), including the cube of 10 (1,000) for absolute completion and perfection.

12. The number representing God's people (12 tribes, 12 disciples) and God at work on the earth (3 x 4), including multiples such as 12,000 and 144,000 for the church made complete.

42 months (11:2). A time of evil and brokenness; 1,260 days in the Jewish lunar calendar; the period of time the two witnesses prophesy in 11:3 and the woman (church) is protected while being pursued by the dragon (Satan) in 12:6. It also equals "a time, times and half a time" (3½ years), during which God will protect the woman (church) in Revelation 12:14. Since these numbers all have the same value and refer to related events, they are best understood to be the same time period referred to in different ways, a technique often used in apocalypses (Daniel 12:7).

1,600 stadia (14:20). A symbolic measurement of the entire earth, determined by taking the number of completion squared (10 x 10) times the number of earth squared (4 x 4); this is equal to the approximate length of Palestine.

144,000 (7:4). The number of absolute completion (10 x 10 x 10) multiplied by the number of God's people (12 x 12); clearly identified in Revelation 14:3 as all those "who had been redeemed from the earth." This is not literally Israel or even Jewish believers; note that the tribe of Manasseh, one of Joseph's sons, is included with Joseph, while the tribe of Dan (see Genesis 49:1–28) is omitted, perhaps due to an association with idolatry (Judges 18:30).

Abaddon and Apollyon (9:11). Both mean "destroyer," describing Satan's purpose.

Abyss (9:1). Hell, the place of the demons, represented by an almost bottomless pit (Luke 8:31).

accuser (12:10). The literal meaning of the name *Satan,* describing how he works to condemn people and separate them from God (Job 1:9–11; Zechariah 3:1).

Alpha and Omega (1:8). Jesus brings about the beginning and the end of the world, represented by the first and last letters of the Greek alphabet (Revelation 1:18; 21:6; 22:13).

Amen (3:14). True; a Hebrew word used to declare the truthfulness of a statement or person (1 Corinthians 14:16).

amillennialism. The view that there is no actual thousand-year period of Christian rule on earth, but that the "thousand" years is symbolic for the entire period from the first coming of Christ until His return.

Antipas (2:13). An otherwise unknown Christian martyr in the church at Pergamum.

apostles (2:2). Those sent out with the authority of Christ, including the original 12 apostles and others sent by the church to preach the Good News (Romans 16:7; 2 Corinthians 11:13).

ark of His covenant (11:19). A symbol of God's presence and faithfulness to His people, the ark held God's law and traveled with His people Israel (Numbers 10:33–36).

Armageddon (16:16). Har Mageddon, literally translated as "the mountain of Megiddo," was a strategic location overlooking a famous battlefield and crossroads, one of the few places large armies could assemble in ancient Israel. Probably not the actual location, but a symbol of massive warfare against God (2 Chronicles 35:20–24).

Babylon the Great (14:8). The enemy of God's people, represented by the capital of Mesopotamia where the Israelites were exiled, a place notorious for luxury and moral corruption (Psalm 137:8; Isaiah 13:19).

Balaam, who taught Balak (2:14). Balaam was infamous as the prophet who helped Balak, king of Moab, in his attempts to curse Israel (Numbers 22:40–25:5; 31:13–16).

beast coming out of the earth (13:11). Religious oppression, or the antichrist, also described as a false prophet (Revelation 16:13; 19:20; 20:10).

beast coming out of the sea (13:1). Political oppression, represented as a wild, dangerous, and hostile figure (Job 40:15–41:34; Daniel 7).

beast . . . from the Abyss (11:7) The force of Satan, the angel of the Abyss (Revelation 9:11).

black horse and rider (6:5). Scarcity as food production is disrupted and trade is imbalanced.

blasphemous name (13:1). An insult to the true God, such as the names of false gods or the title "Lord and God," which the Roman Emperor Domitian assumed (Revelation 17:3).

blood flowed . . . high as the horses' bridles (14:20). All unbelievers died and were judged in a scene of unimaginable horror, similar to that in the apocryphal book 1 Enoch 100:1–3.

bodies will lie in the street (11:8). People will refuse to show any respect, even in death. To refuse a person burial is an ultimate insult in the Middle East.

book of life (3:5). God's record of those made righteous and saved from hell (Psalm 69:28; Philippians 4:3; Revelation 13:8; 17:8; 20:12, 15; 21:27).

bound him for a thousand years (20:2). God limited Satan's power for a complete period of time, the time from Jesus' resurrection until Satan is released to be destroyed at the final judgment (Jude 6).

breastplates of iron (9:9). Armor to protect from counterattack.

breath of life from God (11:11). The resurrection of the witnesses of the church is accomplished through God's Spirit (Genesis 2:7; Ezekiel 37:5, 10).

bride (19:7). God's people, the church (Isaiah 62:5; Jeremiah 2:2; John 3:29; Revelation 21:2, 9; 22:17).

bring her to ruin (17:16). Governments and armies that supported the false religious establishment will despise and turn against it, bringing destruction and humiliation as agents of God's judgment.

burning sulfur (14:10). Fire and brimstone, conferring final judgment on God's enemies (Genesis 19:24; Ezekiel 38:22–23) and the ongoing torment of hell (Revelation 19:20; 20:10; 21:8).

censer (8:3). A container of burning coals used to burn incense, representing the storing of prayers (Revelation 8:5).

clean, shining linen (15:6). A covering of righteousness and glory (Revelation 19:8).

clusters of grapes (14:18). Unbelievers, whose lives gave fruit to the wine of spiritual unfaithfulness (Revelation 14:8) and the wine of God's wrath (Revelation 14:9–10).

coming with the clouds (1:7). Christ's returning to judge the living and the dead (Matthew 24:30; 1 Thessalonians 4:17).

commit adultery (2:22). Often refers to idolatry, not just sexual immorality (Jeremiah 3:6; Hosea 1:2).

covered with eyes (4:6). Able to see everywhere at once, nothing escapes their attention (Ezekiel 1:18).

crown of life (2:10). A symbol of victory over death (James 1:12).

crown of twelve stars (12:1). A crown of victory (2 Timothy 2:5), or angels who fight for all the churches (Revelation 1:20).

crowns of gold (4:4). Represent victory, righteousness, and eternal life given to all believers who persevere in faith (2 Timothy 4:7–8; James 1:12).

dash them to pieces like pottery (2:27). Quickly judge and easily destroy all that is sinful, as when a potter shatters defective pottery (Psalm 2:7–9; Isaiah 30:12–14).

defile themselves with women (14:4). To worship false gods, which were often associated with prostitution in the ancient world (Isaiah 57:3–9; Jeremiah 5:7; Hosea 4:10–13).

desert (12:6). A place of safety, exile, and testing (John 11:54; Revelation 12:14).

door standing open in heaven (4:1). An opportunity for John to glimpse heaven and see the world as those in heaven do (Luke 13:23–25; Acts 14:27).

double-edged sword (1:16). God's Word, with the power to judge and restore (Ephesians 6:17; Hebrews 4:12).

dressed in white (3:4). Cleansed of sin and covered by Christ's righteousness (Isaiah 61:10; Galatians 3:27; Revelation 7:13–14) and eternal life (1 Corinthians 15:53; 2 Corinthians 5:2–3).

eagle (8:13). A sharp-sighted messenger of God, flying above the first four disasters (Isaiah 40:31).

earth . . . swallowing the river (12:16). A miraculous rescue by God, who uses creation to defeat Satanic attacks (Numbers 16:26–32).

earthquake (6:12). The end of the world on the Judgment Day of the Lord, described also in Ezekiel 38:19; Joel 2:31; 3:14–16; Isaiah 13:9; Haggai 2:6; Matthew 24:29; Mark 13:24–25.

Egypt (11:8). The infamous place of Israel's slavery and a source of idolatry (Exodus 2:23; Ezekiel 20:7–8).

eternal gospel (14:6). The Good News of salvation in Christ, which brings eternal life to all who believe.

Euphrates (9:14). The longest river in western Asia, often marking the boundary between Israel and enemies to the east; perhaps represents a point from the beginning of the earth (Genesis 2:14).

exclude the outer court (11:2). Just as Gentiles could occupy the outer court of the temple, so pagan nations will be allowed to persecute God's people on the outside—though true, inner worship will be preserved.

eyes like blazing fire (1:14). Intense, pure, and powerful—the eyes of God (Daniel 10:6; Revelation 2:18; 19:12).

face like the sun (1:16). Having the glory of God, blinding to the human eye (Revelation 21:23).

faithful witness (1:5). Jesus, who reveals the truth about God (John 8:18).

false prophet (19:20). Another name for the harlot or religious beast (Revelation 16:13; 20:10).

fatal wound . . . healed (13:3). The staying power of evil authorities, who return even when thought to be dying, as did the Roman Emperor Caligula (A.D. 37–41).

feet like bronze glowing (1:15). Intense, pure, and strong, perhaps reminding readers of the two massive bronze pillars that framed the temple built by Solomon (2 Kings 25:17).

fiery red, dark blue, and yellow as sulfur (9:17). May refer to colors worn by Roman troops, or may indicate the riders' authority as the fire and sulfur of God's judgment.

fire . . . from their mouths (11:5). God gives His two witnesses the power to call down God's judgment and consuming wrath (2 Samuel 22:9; Jeremiah 5:14).

fire, smoke and sulfur that came out of their mouths (9:18). Authority to produce devastation, death, and destruction as a sign of God's wrath.

firstborn from the dead (1:5). Jesus is resurrected from the tomb so that we also will rise (Colossians 1:18).

firstfruits (14:4). A gift of the first and best of a harvest, given to God as an act of worship, recognizing that the whole crop belongs to Him (Exodus 34:26; 2 Chronicles 31:5; Romans 8:23; 1 Corinthians 15:20).

first love (2:4). Passion and priority given to Christ, as when one first falls in love.

first resurrection (20:5–6). The spiritual resurrection of believers through faith (Romans 6:1–8; Ephesians 2:4–6; 1 Peter 2:24), by which their spirits reign in heaven even before the physical resurrection.

five months (9:5). A temporary period, perhaps modeled on the life cycle of locusts (Revelation 9:10).

four angels who are bound (9:14). Agents of God's judgment, held back until the end of the world, when they will release the power of a massive war in a final attempt to turn unbelievers left on earth back to God.

four living creatures (4:6). Angelic beings who guard the heavenly throne, do God's bidding, and continually worship Him; similarly described by Ezekiel (1:5–10) and called seraphs by Isaiah (6:1–3).

frogs (16:13). Demonic spirits misleading people to serve Satan, the political beast, and the false church, as frogs conjured by magicians misled Pharaoh (Exodus 8:2–7).

full strength (14:10). Not tempered by mercy, as wine was often mixed with water. In the past God held back the complete destruction evildoers deserve, but no more.

futurists. Those who believe that the events described in Revelation have not yet happened, though the persecutions during the Roman Empire gave a preview of struggles to come at the end of the world.

Gog and Magog (20:8). All the unbelieving people, represented by Gog, prince of Meshech and Tubal, and Magog, his tribe, who arouse God's anger by attacking His people and are destroyed (Ezekiel 38–39).

golden sashes (15:6). A sign of honor and dignity bestowed by a king (Exodus 28:40).

gold refined (3:18). True righteousness that withstands God's judgment, as pure gold is separated from impurities by extreme heat (1 Corinthians 3:12–15; 1 Peter 1:7).

great city . . . where also their Lord was crucified (11:8). Literally Jerusalem or figuratively the church, depicted here as immoral, idolatrous, and persecuting the righteous.

great supper of God (19:17). The gathering of birds to eat the corpses of God's enemies, in contrast to the wedding feast of the Lamb; a shocking but fitting judgment on those who persecuted believers (Psalm 79:1–2).

great tribulation (7:14). Troubles and persecutions of believers, especially leading up to the end of the world (Daniel 12:1; Mark 13:19).

had charge of the fire (14:18). Authority to work God's judgment (Revelation 8:3–5).

Hades (1:18). The place of the dead, the Greek word for hell (Matthew 16:18).

hailstones (16:21). Another sign of God's final judgment, which cannot be escaped by running away from the cities (Exodus 9:23; Ezekiel 13:10–14).

harp (5:8). A stringed instrument used to accompany the singing at God's throne (Revelation 14:2; 15:2–3).

harvest of the earth (14:15). The gathering of all people for judgment, believers and unbelievers together, at the end of the world (Matthew 13:24–30, 36–43).

heads of lions (9:17). Images of ferocity and savagery in attacking and killing.

hidden manna (2:17). The mysterious bread from heaven that sustained Israel in its desert wanderings; may suggest a secret source of divine strength or Jesus as the bread of life (John 6:30–58).

His right hand (1:16). God's hand of justice and might upholds the angels of the seven churches, indicating that He is protecting them (Exodus 15:6).

historicists. Those who believe that the visions in Revelation describe events in church history from Christ's first coming to His return—some fulfilled in the days of Rome; others still to come.

home for demons (18:2). An empty and desolate waste, like hell itself.

horns of the golden altar (9:13). Projections resembling animal horns at the corners of the temple altars where those fleeing judgment could find mercy (1 Kings 1:50–51).

horses and riders (9:17). Like the cavalry, a fast-moving and unstoppable army.

human faces (9:7). Having human intelligence and cunning.

hurled it on the earth (8:5). The casting of the censer to earth, with thunder, lightning, and an earthquake. This event connects God's judgments on the earth with the prayers of His people for justice.

idealists. Those who believe that the visions in Revelation aren't of actual events but are symbolic portrayals of the timeless struggle between good (the church) and evil (Rome).

incense (5:8). The prayers of the saints (Psalm 141:2).

in the Spirit (1:10). John was set free from the limits of time and space through the power of the Holy Spirit, taken out of the physical world to experience the spiritual world (Revelation 4:2; 17:3; 21:10).

iron scepter (2:27). Authority that cannot be broken, predicted of the Messiah (Psalm 2:7–9; Revelation 12:5), claimed by Christ (Revelation 19:15), and shared with His people (Revelation 2:26).

jasper . . . carnelian . . . emerald (4:3). God's glory is described in terms of the reflected beauty of precious stones because no one can bear to look at God's brilliance directly. The three stones are among those used to describe the foundations of the New Jerusalem, since paradise is built on God's glory (Revelation 21:19–20).

Jezebel (2:20). A woman of notorious wickedness, she was the idolatrous wife of King Ahab, who introduced the worship of Baal to Israel and killed the true prophets of God (1 Kings 21:25–26).

key of David (3:7). The authority to open or close the kingdom of heaven as the Messiah descended from King David (Revelation 1:8), represented by the same image used to confer authority over Judah to Eliakim (Isaiah 22:20–22).

key to the Abyss (20:1). Authority to lock Satan in hell, though Satan will be released shortly before the final judgment (Revelation 9:1).

lake of burning sulfur (19:20). Hell, the place of permanent destruction (Revelation 20:10; 21:8); also known as the lake of fire (Revelation 20:14–15).

Lamb (5:6). Christ, the Messiah, represented as the perfect lamb, sacrificed for the sins of the world, as predicted in Isaiah 53:7 and identified in John 1:29; 1 Corinthians 5:7; 1 Peter 1:18–19.

legs . . . like fiery pillars (10:1). A reminder of God's presence and protection in dark times, like the cloud and pillar of fire that led Israel in the desert (Exodus 13:21).

leopard . . . bear . . . lion (13:2). Three predators that come out of the sea, in reverse order in Daniel 7:4–6, to represent the Greek, Persian, and Babylonian Empires.

lightning . . . thunder (4:5). Display the power and majesty of God in judgment (Exodus 9:23) and in warning (Exodus 19:16–17). God's voice is often described as sounding like thunder (John 12:29–32).

like a son of man (14:14). Representing Christ, who called Himself the Son of Man (Mark 8:31), and who will fulfill the vision of Daniel 7:13 by "coming with the clouds of heaven" and harvesting believers (Matthew 24:30).

like a thief (3:3). Suddenly and unexpectedly (Matthew 24:42–44; 1 Thessalonians 5:2–4; 2 Peter 3:10; Revelation 16:15).

like crowns of gold (9:7). The appearance, but not the reality, of victory.

like the roar of a lion (10:3). Loud, authoritative, threatening (Proverbs 19:12; 20:2).

Lion of the tribe of Judah (5:5). Christ, the Messiah, predicted in Genesis 49:9–10, where Judah's descendants are given the right to rule "until He comes to whom it belongs and the obedience of the nations is His." Jesus' mother, Mary, and stepfather, Joseph, were both of the tribe of Judah (Isaiah 11:1, 10; Luke 2:4).

lions' teeth (9:8). Ferocity and savagery in attack (Joel 1:6).

little scroll (10:2). A limited revelation, but seen by the whole world (Revelation 10:9–10).

Living One (1:18). Not a pagan, dead god, but a God who lives for all eternity (Joshua 3:10; Psalm 42:2; 84:2).

locusts (9:3). Demons, represented by the terrible plague of insects that could cover a land and destroy all food (Joel 1:1–2:11). Instead of vegetation, these locusts are given power to sting unbelievers.

Lord's Day (1:10). Sunday, the day when Christians celebrate Christ's resurrection (Acts 20:7).

lukewarm (3:16). Apathetic, without passion either for or against God. The attitude of the Laodiceans is neither refreshing, like cool water, nor healing, like the hot springs of nearby Hierapolis.

many waters (17:1). All the peoples, nations, and languages of the earth (Revelation 17:15).

mark . . . of the beast (13:17). Identification as a person devoted to a false god, in contrast to the seal of Christ. Though religious tattoos were common in John's day, the mark is not necessarily physical.

measure the temple (11:1). God's promise to rebuild His relationship with humanity and restore perfect worship is so certain it already can be described in detail and literally counted on (Ezekiel 40:2–5; Zechariah 2:1–5).

Michael (12:7). An archangel (Jude 9) described as the defender of God's people (Daniel 10:13, 21; 12:1).

millennium. Literally a 1,000-year period of time. The belief in a period of time in which Satan will be bound and believers will reign with Christ. There are three different views on when the millennium occurs (see lesson 6).

miraculous signs (13:13). False miracles used to deceive people, such as those used by Pharaoh's magicians (Exodus 7:22).

moon under her feet (12:1). Authority over any lesser power, as the moon is less than the sun (Genesis 37:9; 1 Corinthians 15:41; Isaiah 30:26). Being under a foot implies submission (1 Kings 5:3; Psalm 8:6; 47:3; Matthew 22:44; Ephesians 1:22; Hebrews 2:7–8).

morning star (2:28). Jesus, whose return brings a new and better time, as the appearance of the morning star signaled to ancient watchmen the arrival of a new day (2 Peter 1:19; Revelation 22:16).

Mount Zion (14:1). Heaven, the eternal dwelling of God with His people, represented by the mountain on which the fortress of Jerusalem was built (Galatians 4:26; Hebrews 12:22–24).

multitude (7:9). Believers of all nations and languages stand before God because they remained faithful and are washed clean by Christ's sacrifice (Revelation 7:14).

mystery (17:5). Something that cannot be known unless revealed (Revelation 1:10; 10:7). Many will not recognize the true identity of Babylon, but God's angel reveals it (Revelation 17:8–18).

new Jerusalem (3:12). Paradise, the dwelling place of believers after the resurrection (Revelation 21:2).

new name (2:17). Implies belonging and a fresh beginning, as through Baptism we are adopted into God's family (Isaiah 62:2; Revelation 3:12; 22:4).

new song (5:9). Praises sung by the redeemed, celebrating a new act of deliverance and blessing by God (Psalm 33:3; 96:1; 98:1; 144:9; Isaiah 42:10; Revelation 14:3).

Nicolaitans (2:6). Followers of Nicolas, who apparently condoned immorality (Revelation 2:15).

number of the beast (13:18). Either the number equivalent to the name of a person acting as an anti-Christian religious beast or the unholy trinity of Satan, opposition, and deception trying to take the place of God.

once was, now is not, and will come (17:8). The political beast that persecutes Christians will reappear after being thought to be dead (Revelation 17:11).

one hour (17:12). A very short time; the length of both the reign and ruin of Babylon (Revelation 18:10, 17, 19).

open door (3:8). Opportunity for salvation to spread (1 Corinthians 16:9; 2 Corinthians 2:12; Colossians 4:3) from Philadelphia.

outside the city (14:20). Outside the place of God's people, the church, who are represented by the city of Jerusalem. Bloodshed inside would defile the city (Hebrews 13:12).

pale horse and rider (6:8). Death followed by the grave, afflicting a quarter of humanity at any given time by such means as violence, famine, plague, and animal attacks—the result of unchecked sinfulness.

palm branches (7:9). An ancient symbol of joy and victory (Leviticus 23:40; John 12:13).

pillar in the temple (3:12). Symbol of strength in the presence of God (1 Kings 7:15–21).

postmillennialism. The view that Christ will return to earth after a symbolic period of Christian rule on earth.

power to shut up the sky . . . to turn the waters into blood (11:6). Drought and poisoned water, the same signs of God's wrath that accompanied the messages of Elijah (1 Kings 17:1) and Moses (Exodus 7:17–21).

priests of God (20:6). Servants allowed to enter God's presence (1 Peter 2:5, 9; Revelation 1:6; 5:10).

premillennialism. The view that Christ will return to earth before a literal thousand-year period of Christian rule on earth.

preterists. Those who believe that the events described in Revelation have already taken place during the Roman persecution of first-century Christians and the decline that followed.

prostitute (17:1). The religious enemy of God's people, a symbol of unfaithfulness (Deuteronomy 31:16; 2 Chronicles 21:11), in contrast to the faithful woman who gave birth to God's Son (Revelation 12:5) and the church, who will be presented to Christ as a bride (Revelation 19:7–8; 21:2–3).

purple (17:4). The color of wealth or royalty, since purple was an expensive dye (Revelation 18:16).

rainbow (10:1). Sign of God's promise to never again destroy the earth by flood (Genesis 9:15–16; Ezekiel 1:28).

rapture. The belief that Christ will return before the end of the world to gather the bodies of dead believers, who will be resurrected, and living believers, who will suddenly disappear from the earth.

red dragon (12:3). "That ancient serpent called the devil, or Satan, who leads the whole world astray" (Revelation 12:9).

red horse and rider (6:4). War and bloodshed, inflicting the sword of judgment on humanity.

reigned with Christ a thousand years (20:4). Sat enthroned and exercised authority as saints in Christ's presence from the time of their death to the physical resurrection and final judgment (2 Timothy 2:11–12).

remove your lampstand (2:5). Take away the prominent position of the congregation before God (Revelation 1:20).

right foot on the sea . . . left foot on the land (10:2). Having power over the whole world (Genesis 1:10; Psalm 95:5; Jonah 1:9; Revelation 7:1–2).

right hand or . . . forehead (13:16). Some, marked on the hand, are unaware of doing Satan's work, while others are marked on the forehead, the place of knowledge, since they are aware of whom they serve.

robed in a cloud (10:1). Concealed by the same means God used to reveal His glory (Exodus 13:21; 14:19–20; 24:15–18; 40:34–35; Numbers 9:15–23; Deuteronomy 31:15–16; Matthew 24:30; Mark 13:26; Luke 21:27).

robe dipped in blood (19:13). Not the blood of enemies about to be slain, but Christ's own blood, in which the saints have washed their robes (Revelation 7:15); displayed as a sin offering for others (Leviticus 8:14–15).

Root of David (5:5). Christ, the Messiah, predicted in Isaiah 11:1 and identified in Romans 15:12 as an offshoot of David's father, Jesse. Through Mary and Joseph Jesus was a branch of Jesse and David's family tree, but Jesus was also their root, having created their ancestors.

ruler of the kings of the earth (1:5). Jesus has power over all earthly rulers (1 Timothy 6:14–16).

Satan's so-called deep secrets (2:24). The experience of evils, such as the idolatry and sexual immorality of Jezebel. These were falsely taught by some as necessary to defeat Satan.

scarlet beast (17:3). The political beast out of the sea (Revelation 13:1–8), in a color usually reserved for the wealthy, though perhaps representing the blood of God's persecuted people (Revelation 12:3).

scroll (5:1). God's plan for history. The image may have reminded readers of the stone tablets inscribed on both sides with the covenant law (Exodus 32:15).

sea (13:1). Chaos, destruction, and evil separating people from God (Genesis 7:23–24; Exodus 14:26–27; Jude 13).

sealed with seven seals (5:1). Completely secure and private, as letters—and Jesus' tomb (Matthew 27:65–66)—were sealed with wax so that no unauthorized person could open them and see inside (Esther 8:8; Isaiah 29:11; Daniel 6:17).

seal on the foreheads (7:3). Just as documents were sealed with wax, so all believers are identified and made secure to protect them in the judgment through God's recognition (Ephesians 4:30; 2 Timothy 2:19).

seal up the message (10:4). Delay speaking until the time is right (Daniel 8:26).

sea of glass, clear as crystal (4:6). An image of peace, beauty, and purity before God's throne, where chaos, destruction, and evil of the world are stilled (Exodus 24:9–10; Ezekiel 1:22). In front of the Jerusalem temple a large basin of water for ritual washing was known as the Sea (1 Kings 7:23–26).

sea of glass mixed with fire (15:2). Peaceful calm (the experience of believers) mixed with the fire of judgment (the experience of unbelievers) before God's throne (Revelation 4:6).

seated on the cloud (14:14). Possessing the authority and glory of God (Revelation 14:16).

second death (2:11). Suffering and destruction in hell (Revelation 20:14; 21:8).

serpent spewed water (12:15). Deception and destruction unleashed by Satan like a flood (Psalm 124:2–5; Isaiah 27:1).

seven crowns (12:3). A sign of authority and false divinity; *diademata* in Greek, as opposed to the word *stephanos,* used for the victory crowns of the woman (Revelation 12:1).

seven eyes (5:6). Complete intelligence and insight, the ability to see everything (Proverbs 15:3).

seven golden lampstands (1:12). The seven churches (Revelation 1:20).

seven heads (12:3). Perfect authority, or perhaps seven (imperfect) Roman emperors (Revelation 13:1; 17:3).

seven hills (17:9). The setting of ancient Rome, representing governments that persecute Christians.

seven horns (5:6). Complete power and strength (Deuteronomy 33:17).

seven kings (17:10). May represent all evil rulers, since they don't match any list of emperors known.

seven spirits [or sevenfold spirit] (1:4). The Holy Spirit, who is able to see, understand, and explain all truths (Zechariah 4:2–10; Isaiah 11:2; John 16:13–15; Revelation 4:5).

seven stars (1:16). Angels (Revelation 1:20).

seven thunders (10:3). The sound of absolute divine judgment (Revelation 8:5; 11:19; 16:18).

sharp sickle (14:14). Power to cut off lives and gather believers, as stalks of ripe grain were cut and gathered by a curved blade at harvest time (Joel 3:12–16; Mark 4:26–29).

silence in heaven (8:1). A dramatic pause that builds anticipation and emphasizes the importance of what is to follow, as when people quiet down before a play or movie is about to begin.

snatched up to God (12:5). Ascended to heaven; in contrast to Satan, who is cast out of heaven.

Sodom (11:8). A notorious place of immorality destroyed by God through fire (Genesis 13:13; 19:1–25; Isaiah 3:8–9).

soiled their clothes (3:4). Intentionally and publicly sinning (Isaiah 64:6; Zechariah 3:3–4).

son (12:5). Jesus, the Son of Mary and the Son of God (Isaiah 9:6; Luke 1:35).

song of Moses (15:3). Not literally what Moses sang after God freed Israel, but the same message: all nations know God alone is holy, glorious, and worthy of worship by the way He saves His people (Exodus 15:1–18).

song of the Lamb (15:3). Not what Jesus sang, but what is sung about Him: all nations know God alone is holy, glorious, and worthy of worship by the way He saves His people (Philippians 2:5–11).

sound of . . . battle (9:9). Power to create fear even before striking.

spit you out (3:16). Reject as distasteful (Job 20:15).

spoke like a dragon (13:11). Deceived people on behalf of Satan. The beast uses false religion to secure worship of the political power that authorizes it, as pagan priests did under Rome and others have done since.

standing in the sun (19:17). Reflecting the glory of Christ (Revelation 1:16; 10:1).

star that had fallen (9:1). Satan. Stars represent angels in Revelation 1:20 and in Jewish tradition. Satan is a fallen angel, inhabiting the Abyss of hell and leading the demons.

stomach turned sour (10:10). The content of the message will bring pain (Job 20:12–14).

strike her children dead (2:23). Not necessarily literal children, but those who follow her ways (Hosea 2:4).

sweet as honey (10:10). The message will bring delight (Ezekiel 3:1–3).

synagogue of Satan (2:9). Jewish people who reject the Christ and persecute Christians (3:9).

tabernacle of the Testimony (15:5). The dwelling of God with His people while the Israelites wandered in the desert; this tent held the testimony of God's law (Exodus 38:21) and was replaced by Christ (Hebrews 9:11–14).

tails and stings like scorpions (9:10). Inflicting severe pain; not necessarily fatal.

tails were like snakes (9:19). Demonic power to injure those who escape being killed in a frontal attack.

tail swept a third of the stars (12:4). Satan took other angels with him in rebellion against God (Revelation 12:9).

take it and eat it (10:9). Grasp and fully digest (comprehend) the contents (Ezekiel 3:1–3).

temple in heaven was opened (11:19). God reveals His holy presence to all people and welcomes believers through the work of Christ on the cross (Luke 23:44–46).

ten crowns on his horns (13:1). Royalty and false divinity supported by complete power.

ten days (2:10). A short, but complete, period of time (Genesis 24:55).

ten horns (12:3). Complete power, dominating all other powers on earth (Revelation 17:3, 12).

ten kings (17:12). Rulers with complete military might who wage war against God's people for the beast.

three and a half days (11:11). A short time of evil celebration, in proportion to the three and a half years the two witnesses preached to the world, but not long enough for the world to forget them.

throw dust on their heads (18:19). A sign of great grief (Job 2:12).

trampled in the winepress (14:20). Crushed by God's judgment, as grapes were stepped on to squeeze out their juice in a large basin (Isaiah 5:1–4; 63:2–6; Joel 3:13).

trample on the holy city (11:2). God's people, as the city of Jerusalem, will be abused for a time.

tree of life (2:7). The source of immortality and healing (Genesis 2:9; 3:22; Revelation 22:2, 14, 19).

trumpets (8:6). Loud instruments used to announce important events, sound warnings, and send signals during times of war (Numbers 10:9).

twenty-four elders (4:4). All believers may be represented by the 12 tribes of Israel in the Old Testament and the 12 apostles of the New Testament.

two horns like a lamb (13:11). The appearance of Christ, the Lamb, with the power of the two witnesses.

two hundred million troops (9:16). A huge, nonspecific number of demons, "twenty thousands times ten thousands" in Greek, twice the "ten thousand times ten thousand" elsewhere in Scripture (Daniel 7:10; Revelation 5:11).

two olive trees; two lampstands (11:4). The two witnesses are described as two olive trees, sources of oil for anointing and light, and two lampstands, which generally represent the people of God (Revelation 1:20).

two witnesses (11:3). The testimony of God's people personified by two individuals, probably Moses and Elijah, who represented the Law and Prophets as witnesses to Jesus' transfiguration (Matthew 17:2–3). According to Jewish law, truth was established by the testimony of two witnesses (Deuteronomy 19:15), so Jesus urged acceptance of His message (John 8:16–18) and sent disciples out in teams of two (Mark 6:7; Luke 10:1; Acts 13:2; 15:39–40). Some also see the two witnesses as representing the Old and New Covenants (Hebrews 12:18–24), the prophets and the apostles (Ephesians 2:19–20), or the messages of Law and Gospel (Romans 8:1–4).

up to heaven in a cloud (11:12). Just as Jesus is resurrected and taken up to heaven, so the faithful witnesses are glorified and taken home to God before the final judgment (Acts 1:9).

voice was like the sound of rushing waters (1:15). Loud, massive, and powerful—the voice of God (Ezekiel 1:24).

wedding of the lamb (19:7). The joyous celebration when the church joins Christ forever in heaven; often portrayed as a wedding feast (Matthew 22:2; 25:1–13; Luke 12:35–36; Revelation 19:9).

what He opens . . . shuts (3:7). Christ alone can open and close the opportunity for salvation (Isaiah 22:22).

where Satan has his throne (2:13). The center of emperor worship and other idolatry.

white horse and rider (6:2). Human conquest, appearing as a savior but resulting in oppression.

white like wool . . . as snow (1:14). Indicates the wisdom, purity, and holiness of the presence of God (Daniel 7:9).

white robe (6:11). Victory and purity through Christ's sacrifice (Revelation 7:9, 14).

white stone (2:17). May signify innocence, referring to the custom of judges declaring a person innocent by casting a white stone into an urn.

wine of God's fury (14:10). Overwhelming judgment on evil, represented by wine because it makes people stagger as though drunk (Isaiah 51:17; Jeremiah 25:15; Psalm 75:7–8).

wine of her adulteries (14:8). Spiritual unfaithfulness to God, represented by wine because it is intoxicating at first but leads to tragic foolishness and remorse (Jeremiah 51:6–7; 1 Thessalonians 5:6–9).

wings of a great eagle (12:14). Divine protection (Exodus 19:4; Isaiah 40:31).

Woe! (8:13). A prophetic warning of disaster that will cause grief (Matthew 23:13–29).

woman clothed with the sun (12:1). God's faithful people, the church, reflecting the radiance of Christ (Luke 1:78–79) as His bride (Isaiah 54:1; 62:5; Jeremiah 2:2; Ephesians 5:25; 2 Corinthians 11:2).

women's hair (9:8). Having human beauty and attractiveness.

Wormwood (8:11). A bitter plant, representing sorrow and disaster.

wrath of the Lamb (6:16). Not the personal anger of God, but the reaction of His holiness against sin; God's rejection of those who reject Christ.

wretched, pitiful, poor, blind and naked (3:17). Though Laodiceans were proud of their worldly wealth, vision treatments, and fine wool, they lacked good works, spiritual insight, and the cover of Christ's righteousness.

write on him the name (3:12). Confer belonging and character (Revelation 14:1).